YOUR JOURNEY TO
ENLIGHTENMENT

Twelve Guiding Principles to Connect With
Love, Courage, and Commitment in the New Dawn

Simran Singh

A division of
The Career Press, Inc.
Pompton Plains, NJ

YOUR JOURNEY TO ENLIGHTENMENT
TYPESET BY DIANA GHAZZAWI
Cover design by Joanna Williams
Printed in the U.S.A.

To order this title, please call toll-free 1-800-CAREER-1 (NJ and Canada: 201-848-0310) to order using VISA or MasterCard, or for further information on books from Career Press.

The Career Press, Inc.
220 West Parkway, Unit 12
Pompton Plains, NJ 07444
www.careerpress.com
www.newpagebooks.com

Library of Congress Cataloging-in-Publication Data
CIP Data Available Upon Request

Praise for *Your Journey to Enlightenment* and Simran Singh

"Simran is one of the most exciting authors, visionaries, speakers, and humanitarians in the world today, and what we can learn from her to add to our own lives is invaluable."

—Michelle Phillips, best-selling author of *The Beauty Blueprint*

"*Your Journey to Enlightenment* offers interesting and fresh insight into the dynamics of letting go, allowing the truth of oneself the full expression of freedom. Simran Singh illustrates, in a simple and compassionate way, how to move through life in full play anchored by love, courage and commitment."

—Anita Moorjani, *New York Times* best-selling author of *Dying to Be Me*

"Simran Singh has written a wise and illumined book on the great evolutionary imperative of our time…. Seekers on all levels will find here sources of sacred passion and joy."

—Andrew Harvey, author of *The Hope* and *Radical Passion*

"*Your Journey to Enlightenment* is a brilliant book. Anyone seeking enlightenment through a path of innocence and child-like simplicity should read this gem from Simran Singh."

—Annie Kagan, author of *The Afterlife of Billy Fingers*

"…a real pro with a big heart and expanded consciousness."

—Jack Canfield, *Chicken Soup for the Soul* series

"*Your Journey to Enlightenment* is a rich, deeply devotional writing of how to live outside the box and in the adventure as life was intended. This is spirited, spiritual writing that opens the doors to true transformation and it is highly recommended."

—Sunny Dawn Johnston, speaker and author of *Invoking the Archangels*

"Simran Singh is a wise woman; she understands the core principles of the nonphysical realms, how they translate into the structure of our physical world, and how our world is changing. We need varying explanations of the transformation process—sometimes all it takes for understanding to click in us is to hear a description that is one degree different from another one. In *Your Journey to Enlightenment*, Singh gives us a fresh roadmap that really makes sense and provides deep comfort."

—Penney Peirce, author of *Frequency* and *Leap of Perception*

"*Your Journey to Enlightenment* is powerfully persuasive and practical in discovering how to embrace freedom. Simran Singh has loaded it beautiful intentions and playful exercises that will change your experience and expression of life forever."

—Ester Nicholson, author of *Soul Recovery*

"Every time this woman speaks, she touches my soul deeply and profoundly. I highly recommend her book. Simran Singh has a way with words that will connect you to your heart and to the heart of the Universe."

—Andrea Henkart, author of *Trust Your Body! Trust Your Baby!*

"Rarely have I heard such wisdom. Outside of the modern day mystics, no one has the courage to speak this truth. I am humbled by Simran's perspectives and have been moved to tears."

—Tom Shadyac, director and author of *Life's Operating Manual*

In dedication to the Divine Child.

May sovereignty rule your experience and creativity be embodied through continuous play as you experience the rebel path of love, courage, and commitment.

In Love, of Love, with Love and Laughter.

Acknowledgments

I would like to express the deepest gratitude to Richard Rudd and Maureen Moss for your beautiful voices and hearts. I cherish you for the profound ways you have impacted my experience.

My love and gratitude to my innermost circle of synarchy, my Rebel Roadies on the unknown path, Kristi Reagor, Naomi Mitsuda, Sage, Krish, and all those along the way that have embodied this Rebel Spirit. Your love, courage, and commitment have been the touchstones we have shared in the most deeply intimate way, and I am truly grateful in sharing this journey with you. Especially deep love, respect, and appreciation to you, Tuckie... Tuck Self. You have been an anchor of immense joy, support, and celebration.

Special gratitude and affection to Sandie Sedgebeer, Jill Mangino, Jill Angelo, Eileen Duhne, Ann Stirling, Ankha Marza, Celeste Merek, Shanel Barney, Honi Borden, Morgan Justus, Laura Tallman, Deb Carraro, Gregory Moye, Nisco, Deanna Walker, Rick Beresford, Peg Zenuga, Tom Dalziel, Rick Batyr, Barry Goldstein, and Gogi Randhawa.

Thank you Bill Gladstone for your commitment to my writing. Deepest gratitude for Laurie Pye, Michael Pye, and the amazing family at New Page. For my radio family, Jeff Gerstyl, Brandy

Jackson, and Voice America 7th Wave, thank you for giving me such a beautiful way to play.

Sage and Krish, thank you for lighting the way in helping me remember. You are Divine children. I wish you an ever-expanding playground upon which to play, dream, create, and experience your magnificence. May you never work a day in your life, and play fearlessly and joyfully throughout eternity.

Contents

Foreword

11

Introduction

13

The Invitation

29

The Invocation

105

The Initiation

145

The Integration

187

The Inspiration

207

The Illumination

225

Invitation From the Author

241

Afterword

245

Index

247

About the Author

253

Foreword

The book you are about to read is a feast of Truths. Simran Singh has poured her heart into every page, and immediately you will see what a great heart she has. In our modern age of accelerated change, there are so many voices clamoring to be heard. Often the voice that is heard the least is the quieter voice of the child, and in this book you will find, above all, the pulsing heart of a child.

Simran presents a vision of the potential of humanity, not as some mysterious league of awakened light beings, but as a race of fully matured, enlightened children. This notion of playfulness dances and shimmers across each page of the text. The elegant and creative structure of the book gives the reader a strong sense of purpose and form, while at the same time, the words loop and curve like the many different faces of a living river. Simran constantly invites us into her heart, through fragments of poetry, praise, prayer, and song. She invites, invokes, and insists on the need for us to empower ourselves.

This is a new kind of book. It is a book bursting with life. Sometimes when reading it, I could almost imagine the words themselves wanting to leap off the page and run off down to the river to play. And such a book needs to be read, I think, in a certain way. Truth does not reveal itself to a frown of concentration. It opens to a lighter touch. I therefore recommend you read this book without expectation and without any sense of pressure. Read it as you would eat an ice cream, without too much care but with a wicked sense of delight. This is clearly how the book was written, and it is clear that Simran wishes us to join her as a friend and equal rather than setting her on any kind of pedestal.

At the same time, this is a serious book. The paradox of Truth demands it embrace both ends of the spectrum. It is serious because it begins by challenging our tendency to see ourselves as the victim. But Simran sees the human Shadow as a bridge to a new kind of consciousness, the awakening of the Creative Rebel. As I read the part of the book that deals with the Shadow, at times in the text I feel deeply uncomfortable; this is how I know the words are authentic. When you feel this discomfort yourself, instead of rushing on to the next part, I suggest slowing down even more. We are all human and we all know the same pain and the same restlessness of spirit. Simran knows it too. And she also knows how to transmute it—how to grow *through* it—rather than remain trapped by it. And then we may follow her example, when we have summoned up enough of a lion's roar in our heart!

So you may count yourself fortunate that this book has fallen into your hands. It may be that Grace had a hand in it. Above all, I hope that you will take pleasure from reading, contemplating, dipping, and diving through its many precious insights. It is a Dionysian book, designed to help bring you closer to your own ecstasy and into the pure-hearted child who is always laughing in your heart.

—Richard Rudd

INTRODUCTION

Do you remember when you transitioned from the label of child to "grown up"? Can you recall that moment when you knew you had stepped into adulthood? Most people do. They remember being children...until they weren't. They remember being adults even more so. Although we carry memories of being children, and perhaps some remnants of it continue, the next phase of life begins at some point, probably too soon. We become the adult—serious, responsible, practical, safe—all part of "the real world."

I grew up fast. I can show you pictures of seriousness at the age of three. I was an adult by the time I was four. My parents had to work very hard to support us, having come to North America with only eight dollars in hand. They were gone most of the time, because they had to provide.

My wheelchair-bound grandmother was there to take care of me, though I actually took care of her. I cleaned up, "gofered," answered the door, got the mail, and helped prepare lunch. I had lots of little tasks. From there, I moved to working in the family business, at the age of eight. If I was not working at my parent's store, I was taking care of my younger brother and sister. I learned how to be responsible, diligent, focused, and very serious early on. By age 12, I had a schedule: school from 7:30 to 3:00, work at the family business from 3:30 to 7, and study from 8:00 to 11:00.

Work did not leave time for friendships or play. I never really learned how to interact with others socially, only in a business manner. I did not learn how to do small talk or have the experience of girlfriends and sleepovers, silliness and dress-up, sisterhood and camaraderie. My parents were protective and felt that I could get into less trouble if I was working beside them. I was quiet and shy, introverted and contemplative. I kept things organized and running smoothly, and I took over tasks as needed. It was not long before I became the queen of multi-tasking and a jack-of-all-trades.

Some might say those moments stood for my love, courage, and commitment. However, if they did, they were based upon the old paradigm of staying safe, in survival mode and gripped with fear. So at that time, these things—love, courage, and commitment— were actually a call for love, a strong will, and cultural, generational, and familial obligation.

As a young woman struggling to remain loyal to my parents, culture, and religion, something within me also desired to expand into the American culture in which I lived and breathed. However, I was very aware from the beginning that I was different. It was pointed out to me repeatedly, so much so that I bought into this concept and isolated myself, piece by piece. These beliefs and the ones that layered, year after year, created an incredible "story," the hero's journey. It began as all great stories do: in fear, darkness, deceit, escape, and control.

Through experiences of prejudice, work-a-holism, several miscarriages, and a semi-arranged marriage filled with abandonment, betrayal, and addiction, I sought refuge in my inner world. I compartmentalized my life, so that the chaos had a nice, safe place to be packed away. I became adept at focusing my attention so that I could develop areas of beauty and creation all around me to balance the ugliness that was present. Although everything serves, I eventually realized these were all masks to some degree—the beautiful, good, bad, and the ugly. As in every costume party, eventually the masks must fall, because what is underneath is very real and desires to be seen and heard.

The falling away of my masks mirrored the falling away of my life—career, relationships, marriage, identity, and beliefs. Initially, it seemed life was pulling these things from me. Then I began to understand that there was no one in the room but me and God. And, unbeknownst to me until much later, God was only giving me what I deeply asked for. The Divine always heard what my depths were crying for, even if I consciously did not. How could I have known all of the experiences around me were showing me... me? I was just trying to figure it all out, trying to bring meaning to my life. In an attempt to understand, the questions formed: "*Why are these things happening? Who am I? Why am I here? When will it end? What is my life's purpose? Does it all have meaning or is this just random?*"

I refused to believe that life was random or that we were thrown into a haphazard Universe. I refused to believe in a God that punished, judged, or became angry. That made no logical sense to me. Something else had to be going on here, and there was only one common denominator: *me!* I knew I had to be a big part of it. I began to realize a relationship existed between my inner landscape and outer world. I noticed a conversation was happening—a *Conversation With the Universe*, the title and essence of my first book speaking to the signs, symbols, and messages the Universe gives all of us in every situation, all of the time.

In noticing the mirrors all around me, I began to see who I had really been and what I really believed about the world. Within those reflections, some of me was really amazing, beautiful, and strong; other parts of me were horrifying, hideous, and weak. I cracked open the door to becoming a whole and healed human being, engaging in deep study, spiritual practices, healing modalities, and self-inquiry. I did the inner work. I was told I was an onion and had layers, so I began peeling back the onion, layer by layer.

I made the decision that there was no one to blame, no one to shame, and no one whose job it was to save me. I knew, without doubt, that my power lay within my pain, and only I could be responsible for my own life and its expression and experience. At that time, I asked myself one question: *"What is it that I really want?"* My response was a very simple one: *"I desire to love and be loved unconditionally. I desired to connect and be an agent of connection. I desired to create beauty in the world and see the beauty of myself."*

In the unfolding process, I discovered the Universe was indeed having a constant conversation with me—everywhere I turned— and it was nothing but loving, completely connected, and amazingly beautiful.

Several years ago, the numbers 11, 111, and 11:11 began appearing all of the time, as many as 20 times a day. When I inquired as to why this was happening, the first issue of *11:11 Magazine*—every word, image, interview, logo, meaning of the logo, sacred geometry, subsequent covers, and radio show titles—was downloaded into my head. Every word and image was vivid and clear.

I was given the message, *"Do this now. You will heal; others will heal."* I said YES, aware that I had no prior experience in publishing or radio. I felt terrified, but knew that I was being guided. I had no idea that each issue was to be a curriculum "devoted to the journey of the soul," to support the wounded human in approaching the gateway for the multi-dimensional Hue-man to emerge and be illuminated.

I began taking bold and courageous leaps to transform my experience. I must admit, I follow direction very well and have an incredible work ethic. I learned how to create whatever the Universe asked of me. If there is one thing for certain, I am completely committed when I focus on something.

All the while, I was growing, changing, evolving, and mastering my experience. However, as I began witnessing parts of me that were truly leaping, there was a subtle feeling of an invisible net that existed. Even though I could not bring words to it, I was caught within it. I could not see it—I could not even feel it—but some part of me knew it was there. It was holding me back from true realization. I also felt a field that surrounded me, a very loving and nurturing essence that was ready to hold me in its full embrace whenever "I chose" to release the net of illusion I was "caught up in."

But, in that moment, I was "too busy" to discern where it was, and a part of me was afraid of truly stepping into my power. It felt immense, greater than I had the confidence of being. It was still safer to pretend I was in my power than to actually be in it. As in all cases, our deepest desires will always rise up so that every misalignment and untruth crumbles away, no matter how hard we struggle to keep them in place. Whether we are ever willing to admit it or not, the Divine power that rests within each one of us is a truth that will not stay suppressed. It will burrow through the core and into life until it is known, owned, and experienced.

I convinced myself, justified, that I was fully in my power. I was creating a beautiful, conscious, inspirational magazine that was reaching people all over the world. I was repeatedly told by best-selling authors appearing on 11:11 Talk Radio and in the pages of

11:11 Magazine that I was the best interviewer they had ever had. I received constant feedback on social media that my posts were dramatically affecting people's lives. My newsletter blog would receive hundreds of replies of gratitude and awareness each week. I was doing my thing, and I do not discount it was having an effect on many in the world. But, everything was crumbling. My life had become very aligned over the years but now everything felt as if it was shrinking. And a part of me still felt something missing.

Do you know that place where everything seems all right, looks good from the outside, is perceived by all others as the dream, but you know there is something that must change? That was where I was: *"Something isn't quite right. This cannot be it! Is this really all there is?"* The life I was living seemed on purpose, but where was my bliss? Where was the radiance?

I could feel the small cracks forming around me. Conversations with the Universe constantly revealed strong messages alerting me to what needed to happen. My dreams were foretelling a great time of change. Then, I chose to experience 11 days of silence in the Sacred Valley of Peru. My intention was to have the Lover and Beloved experience, a communion with God deeper than I had ever known. And I did. My time in silence, profound to say the least, let me see what was trying to crumble away. This new Golden Age was asking more of me, more of us, to truly live as radiant, multi-dimensional beings of Light in full brilliance.

Upon returning from Machu Picchu, I knew my 18-year semi-arranged marriage was complete. Eighteen years prior, we had each consented to follow Indian tradition, allowing our parents to choose our life partner. I had never dated and had told my parents I would marry whomever they chose. My husband followed tradition to be a role model to his younger brothers. Mutual friends of the family introduced us, and we were married.

Eighteen years later, I knew we had fulfilled our soul contract to one another and had grown all that we could in each other's presence. I could see that very clearly. It was time for both of us to move on if we were to continue to evolve.

I knew I had to be the one to leap. I had fought this action for many years, not wanting 'not wanting to be "that" person who left. This was my mask, a false version of love, courage, and commitment to stay out of my own power and to uphold an identity. I preferred to stay within what I knew was hard, even if uncomfortable and painful. It was scary. It could get lonely. I was loving...everyone else. I was being committed to everything else but my own life. I had never had the courage to leave.

It was very clear. I was in that old paradigm of staying safe, surviving, and resting in fear of the unknown. My choice, either way, would have a profound impact on the experience and expression of the rest my life.

I also knew that *11:11 Magazine* was complete. The experience of Lover and Beloved would be the final issue. I understood the grandness and necessity of the letting-go process. This 11:11 identity of mine was releasing so that I could make space for something new, something completely unknown to me. The time had come to break through all glass ceilings. I could feel something happening inside and outside, something bigger than "I." All I could do was wait in the void, wait for the next step to be revealed, flirting and playing with what life placed in my sight, literally in my grasp.

The third thing that occurred from my journey to Peru was a youthfulness awakened in me. It was as if an adolescent had just discovered love for the first time. I wanted to dive into what was in front of me with all the zest, reckless abandon, and passion surging inside. Something compelled me to experience myself in this way while I waited in the void. That love, the passion and joy I felt, the excitement that was a completely foreign experience, energized me completely. I wanted more and more of that in my life. And, I could see that, in letting myself have it, life was expanding in response.

It is amazing what happens when you go with what the Universe is offering and asking. The conversation began as signs, symbols, and synchronicities woven together to create vast sentences of direction and action. I completely let go of my mind, all responsibility and sensibility, and followed my heart into response-ability and sense-ability, both distinctly different than the aforementioned. I was in the YES for what was being asked of me. That YES was engaging an experience of communion and union in life different than I had ever known. When that much love is poured on anything, everything unlike it must rise up and out so that we are given opportunity to know the timeless, boundless ecstasy that is the Divine inheritance.

My divorce occurred six months faster than scheduled. I was led to enter into a contract on a home where I could raise my two boys in a "practical" manner. As usual, the Universe was not sparse on conversation. The home was on Rebellion Road. It was a perfect square, exactly aligning to the feng shui bagua map. There was an atrium in the very center of the home that led to the sky. In the bagua map, the center of the square is the place to center and connect in spirituality from the earth's core to the high heavens. Even the numbers of the house were a strong message of what was to unfold spiritually and globally for me. Everything—every thing—lines up and speaks for us, as us, to us. Everything means something; everything is a message for the next step, a Conversation with the Universe.

I spent several months giving myself the space to move through the changes that were happening. I gave myself rest and space. I knew I would be guided when the time was right. I needed only be present, so that I could be aware of the signs and messages as they appeared. It was not long before the pieces began to come together. I began having glimpses and a knowing of a me I did not know.

Ironically, in the initial vision, I had been guided to go into spiritual comedy. This is funny in itself, since I did not have a funny bone in my body. But I said yes. Upon doing so, Maureen Moss, President of One World Puja Network, at the time, invited me to do a show. I offered them "On the Lighter Side," because I did not want to repeat the type of show I had on 11:11 Talk Radio on VoiceAmerica. It would be my foray into funny—not that I was. But perhaps the intention was to find my funny and teach people how to find theirs along the way. The network loved the idea.

But then, in a meditation, I was given the message to do a one-woman show with story, humor, and song: The Rebel Road: Connecting the Dots of What Was to What IS. Really? *Really?* What was the Universe thinking? Had it dived into a black hole? Had I lost my mind? Was I actually contemplating this?

Well...this was going to be interesting, considering I also never sang before. How was I going to learn to do all of that in a six-month period? Furthermore, I was to write an album of songs that were part of this show I was to put on in 66 cities across North America, from August 2013 through June 2014. Despite every logical cell in my body, I said *"YES."* It is not that I am a thrill-seeker. I am simply a soul in complete devotion to the Beloved.

On the day of my divorce proceedings, I sat in the warm embrace of the sun and fell into a deep meditation. I was given glimpses of the net I had chosen not to see all these years. I was stepping deeper into the human condition, or shall I say human conditioning—the justifications, practicalities, reasons, and excuses, the trap that most of us succumb to. These justifications keep us from our dreams and our passions. I realized that the excuses have a variety of faces:

- "I can't do that; I have kids."
- "I am single; I have to be responsible."
- " I am married; my partner would never support this."
- "I am too old."
- "I am too young."
- "I am too sick."
- "I do not have the money to do this."
- "What about all the years I spent getting my degree?"
- "I have built up a career and now I am just supposed to leave it for a pipedream?"
- "I have people to worry about and care for."
- "There is no time for me."
- "There is not enough time."
- "I don't know how."

The list of excuses is endless. And I was about to do it again, but for the first time in my life, I was conscious that excuses existed. I had "settled" in life. My practical justifications of buying a house and keeping my kids safe in a "normal" life were some of these very excuses. I had settled—in my life, in my marriage, in my relationships, in my career, in my self. My whole life had been a settling process.

In that moment, I realized I was not buying the house. Like everything, it simply appeared, as a message; it did not mean I needed to own it. I was trying to attach to something that was just passing through as guidance and symbolism. It was merely to be an experience and a YES. I called my realtor and told her to cancel the contract. It was still under the due diligence time period and easily dissolved. But regardless of that, the lessons from the experience did not escape me. This purchase was to be the beginning of a whole new list of excuses in my life so that I did not stand in full radiance and power. I had to discover what was beyond me, beyond practicality and linear living.

Buying the home was out of integrity with the message of The Rebel Road tour. The mission of this show was to let people know they have no excuse to not live their hearts' desires, their passions, their dreams, what fills their souls. There are absolutely no excuse good enough! Yet, are these not the excuses we use to limit ourselves—to hinder, to hide, to squash, to suppress, to blame, to shame, to belittle...to regret?

I was to be the example, as I had been so many times before. It was how my Message, my Mastery, my Ministry had always been shared, by being real, openhearted, and vulnerable. However, this was different territory. It was easy to be real, open, and vulnerable about a story that I knew. Could I be open and vulnerable about the me that had yet to reveal? This would be a stretch, internally and externally, personally and professionally, humanly and spiritually. I stood solid in my YES. And as always, in saying YES to the soul, to service, and to the greatest go(o)d, the doors of all-possibility open.

What lined up? I began being downloaded with material for a book, a curriculum or path for returning to multidimensional expansive living. New Page Books contacted my agent requesting I write a book on exactly what this book is about: the path to unfolding the new human. This was not only to be theory or simply written about, but also lived and proven. In this moment, I am living proof of what you are reading, a clear channel of experience.

Synchronicity immediately began appearing. My first book was scheduled to release the day before TedxCharleston, where I was selected to speak. Finally, a major TV network conveyed interest in doing a reality show on the tour. Individuals came forward to volunteer in being a part of The Rebel Road.

That same energy has led you to now read it, as thousands upon thousands have been witnessing it through the tour. I would venture to say there is a very ancient, deep part of you that is ready to take The Rebel Road.

There is one essential message here. You are no longer wounded; that is "story." You are a Master. You have always been. It is time to awaken to that truth of you. Move beyond the smoke and mirrors, the layers of veils and the incredible story you created. It is time to be the rebel in your own life. It is time for you to live a life of love, courage, and commitment as you step into the New Dawn.

"RISE...RADIATE...SHINE...ILLUMINATE!

You are vibration, sound and Light...

You are the Light-Man Cometh...

Light-Womb-Man Cometh.

Sweet and powerful Rebel, what say you?"

Special Note

Certain words and phrases or sentence structures are being used within the book, especially within invitations and activations, to unlock certain parts of you to greater degrees of your Light. Take these areas into contemplation, especially if they cause you to pause, question, or desire to fix.

There are also sacred shapes of Light and high frequency intentions that, if meditated on or simply looked at, will create remembering within your cellular structure.

Specific forms of play are provided to take you back to something you know inherently. Sit at a playground while you read some, or all, of this book. Literally, let yourself play as a child, on that playground. Watch the little children who are present as they play. They know the secrets. Watch and learn from our true Master Teachers. We birth them—their primary intention is to rebirth each of us—because we forgot who we are. Let us not mistakenly give them amnesia.

Light continually comes in, as, and through us. See how it plays with you. You are already blessed. Now BE the blessing.

I am the dream awakening.
I am a spark, a Divine ONE.
My brilliance lights up the world.
My radiance is the dew/due of creation.
I am the Divine Masculine that seeds ideas.
I am the Divine Feminine that nurtures and rears them.
I am the Divine Child here to engage with them.
I am the Divine giggle that sustains them.
I am the connective Golden thread to all things
birthing, shifting, and evolving.
I am the space of the unknown, waiting to become known.
I am the experience and expression of love, courage, and
commitment being Divine Essence in play.

The truth is out!

THE INVITATION

We are at a churning point in humanity's journey, not a turning point. A churning point is a place of agitation. Settling deeply beneath the surface, this palpable tension is a buildup of generations upon generations being conditioned to believe we are less than we really are. This rising within is stirred by the wake-up calls of our time. As the systems of our world crumble around us, it may feel safer to retreat into these old ways of survival, fear, and isolation. It may sound practical to hold back and be cautious. It may really make sense to not ruffle any feathers or stir up the waters. These would be the answers if your intention is to stay limited, stuck, confined, enslaved, and unconscious.

Although the gravity rests within the enormous risk to our collective well-being, settling for what we believe we have been dealt individually is how the churning began in the first place. Now more than ever, there is even greater risk to not living out the true, authentic nature and power that has been hidden, forgotten, and deeply suppressed as familial pathology. This power and knowing is steeped in our cells and is rising, in fact swelling, beneath the churning.

Yes, it feels like agitation. At times, the skin feels tight around the body. There is a sense that the energy running through the physical body cannot contain itself. Many might mistake that for modern-day stress. However, it is something very different. The agitation is a shake-up—a lifting, in fact. It is likened to a snake shedding its skin. As we rub up against uncomfortable or threatening circumstances—the rough patches—the skin that binds will eventually shed. The sharp points of life are tearing at it so that the bigger beingness of who we are may have an opportunity to emerge. But it requires our movement, the willingness to twist and turn, expanding beyond our own self-imposed boundaries.

This is the opening moment of cellular realization that so much of what we believe ourselves to be is a lie or a very grand distortion of the truth. The tightness is experienced because a deep knowing is surfacing; we are bigger than the vehicle being inhabited. We are more connected than simply the things we touch with the body. The truth of who we are cannot be confined. The stress is the tension of conformity. And for each person, a moment shall happen when they say, *"No more. This is not who I am! This is not how my life was meant to be. This is not the manner in which I choose to live any longer. I rebel!"*

Human conditioning has created varied forms of the "Stepford human." This cannot sustain. The falsehoods we have come to follow can no longer sit lodged inside of our systems. This is a dissonant vibration that reveals itself as something that might look like fear, but it has the opportunity to be so much more. This is truly an awakening, not one we wait for. It is not awakening by some outside force. This awakening, present here and now, is one to be consciously invited and invoked. Each individual's awakening must be a self-initiated and cell-abrated integration! We must inspire it, becoming self-illumined and claiming the gifts we have always had.

The awakening from human to Hue-man requires we move from the references of "what was" to the presence of "what IS." The only importance for "what was" is to create the initial bridge one must cross, as they let go of the greatest illusion of all: the inheritance of woundedness from generations, held beliefs systems, entities of stuckness and attachment, to emotion and experience. It is letting go of the idea that we are mere humans in a vertical time line, composed of what has compounded in the past. Instead, we are the creative expression of Divinity in a playground that holds no time, only space in a horizontal configuration, all of which exists now.

"Hue-man" is the light ray embodiment that every individual brings in as individuation of Divinity expressing in, as, and through each one of us. We see ourselves as physicality, but in actuality, we are energy light-streams of sound and color. We are multi-dimensional in nature, reawakening to the fullness of that radiant embodiment. It is also the recognition and acknowledgement of that Light and natural Essence of Divinity that we express as. We each hold a sacred genius and style; our Light body reflects that. The Divine ray of color each person streams sheds Light onto life for experience to experience itself as a unique piece of the puzzle—unique in creation and creativity, but the same in capacity and ability.

It is time to release the idea that we live and then we die. We must purge ourselves of the beliefs that we are subject to any dogma—political, religious, social or otherwise, even the dogmatic interpretations of universal law.

In stepping across this bridge of consciousness, we are beckoned to look at who we are being. We are asked to gauge how we are doing. We are being teased into aliveness, something few have truly known. It is time to make the conscious choice to leap into unknowing. We have had decades where we chose to continually look back in order to move forward. We needed to know. The mind had to figure it out and the body required something to do, something that made sense and filled the time. That is not who we are; it has never been. It is why life has never seemed to fully work.

Why are so many people having the "state of our world" conversation? Multiple voices around the globe continually bring attention to the plights we face in this moment, in hopes to awaken those that slumber. They are asking us to be aware, to make choices, to respond, to act on behalf of our children, humanity, and Mother Earth. But they are asking humans who are holding the baggage of the human condition to also carry the weight of fixing the erupting chaos that appears everywhere.

Are we to stop what is happening? Is that the solution? How exactly is that to happen? Are we to clamor about and demand change? Are these conversations birthing the innovation fast enough? Is there a missing piece? Or are we not accessing our Truth resources?

The past taught us to be revolutionary. We have been shown how to fight in war and fight for peace, but fight nonetheless. Revolutions are a reaction to circumstances, not necessarily resolutions to them. For a new experience of humanity and the awakening to being Hue-man, we must choose something radically different.

The fact is, the crumbling is good. Our world falling apart is in Divine Order; it cannot be otherwise. This Universe is set up as a self-organizing system. What is happening in politics, economics, healthcare, relationships, and even religion, is the process of systems righting themselves. We are part of that natural order that organically self-organizes. It is time to right ourselves as well.

We have become as outmoded as the systems that are crumbling. We have been fighting the changes on the outside, and equally fighting the changes on the inside. The human being and the manner in which it has functioned will not be able to survive if we continue being whom we have been, doing as we have done, living how we have lived, or basing our choices on what we knew. The greatest weakness is the perception though which we view ourselves, through which we know ourselves.

It is easy to want to stand against and fight what we see. It is also easy to acknowledge where we are and that something must change. But that is still just being an observer. We must change. But in what way? Revolution storms against society, against economic structure, against religion, against the government and politics. Revolutionaries fight the systems in place; they rest in a negative state of creation. They are fueled by the power to protest. Revolutionaries demand, by force. This is no time for a revolution. But it may very well be a time for rebel-lion, a Rebel fully committed to living the unknown, a lion here to roar and be king of its own existence and creation.

It is time to become the Rebel, one who is willing to stand in his or her uniqueness, completely living beyond the firms and functions of existing societal paradigms. It is one who desires to be a pioneer, innovative and creative. The Rebel stands ready for experience and the ongoing expansion of being experience experiencing itself. A Rebel's action comes out of their deepest silence and spontaneity. It is not of the mind. It can only be from the radical passion of the heart and soul. The Rebel knows only adventure, living in the YES that is the precursor to action. The Rebel creates, giving birth to the self via constant passionate experience. This is the new man, the Hue-man. Heralding a new age, the Hue-man creates in all-possibility, allowing access to unknown dimensions, within and without.

Your steps toward accepting the gifts that are within you and awakening to the Hue of your Divine Power is the road that will unleash a multi-dimensional experience of you. This new way of being will allow for a more panoramic view of life, rather than using tunnel vision to look at it. Tunnel vision has had you running all over the place trying to reach one fixed destination. Tunnel vision has had you on a journey instead of the panoramic view of being the journey. The panorama allows you to experience all the possibilities creation has for you, as you, and presents a path of synchronicity and symbolism that can be followed.

As I progressed through my divorce process, I felt this churning going on within me. My skin kept tightening as I became more and more aware of what I had allowed my life to become. I was a caged bird. I had never flown free. I had known little more than work. I woke up each day, attended to my children, worked, attended to my children, and went to bed. Even when my husband had been part of my life, he was not around. I had nothing to do, so I worked. I had not learned how to be comfortable with people because my conversations seemed to make them uncomfortable: I desired substance; they wanted to gossip. I desired vulnerability and openness; they wore masks and gritted their teeth behind sweet smiles. I wanted to have fun, laugh, dance, and play, but this did not seem like what people did. Was I born in the wrong place? At the wrong time? With the wrong people? Or, was this churning asking me to allow myself a new experience for the better of all?

Find your calm. Let silence and determination see beyond the illusion of chaos and confusion. This is the mystery, and only in this sphere can you awaken to your Mastery. Be aware of everything around you and imagine yourself seeing the secrets of life. You have come from a turbulent past and are heading to an uncertain, yet hopeful future. You must flow with the times and be a dynamo of direction when you are called upon, knowing the Universe is in full support and conversation with you.

Be clear in your vision, and have the unyielding focus and the patience to see all matters to the end. In an impatient world, patience would be likened to compassion. Compassion and "come-passion" both stem from the heart space. Patience does not come from the will you have always had, but instead the willingness you may personify. Unless your core has been given the foundation of a pure and open heart, the will can exhaust and the fumes of depletion and human conditioning will filter back in. Willingness is the open space of experience that has the ability to create boundless energy through the excitement of discovering the unknown self and its capabilities for creation.

Be aware of all the power you have. A key factor is the cultivation of a strong inner life, an inner authority. This is a delicate and gently unfolding romance, but with a deep faith that unravels many secrets, where you will see all your desire come to pass. Be willing to be Lover and Beloved and create an awakening inside and out. Are you willing? Are you ready? Does everything in your life tell you it is time to allow more than you ever have before?

Your clinging to an identity is your lack of identity. Don't be surprised if there are two people in you now, the familiar face that comes and goes through the world and another face, perhaps one you don't even know yet. This is the one inviting you. You are not in the world. You are not of the world. You are the world and the discovery of that. You are experience experiencing itself—formless, timeless, boundless creative capacity.

An invitation awaits you to discover what has been hidden from you all along. Has it been a conspiracy? Yes. You conspired for this time. It is the final walk of the Divine journey, when the dawn comes and there is Light. The surprise, however, is that the Light is not to shine upon you; it is to brilliantly radiate from within you. You are Light, Vibration, Sound, and Energy, here to be seen, felt, heard and expressed.

This is not pressure to do or be anything. This is an invitation, to be accepted or denied. You are the ONE invited. But, you must be the ONE that extends the invitation. And YOU would be the ONE that accepts it.

≈

You are Grace-fully Invited to the Essence of
Divine Unveiling

Be decked in Beautiful Rebelry and

Full sensory, Multi-dimensional Experience.

The Illumination of Being is to Dance in

Pleasure—Adventure—Freedom—Gratitude—
Transparency—Expression

Revealing the Magyck of Your Soul Song Awakening

Completing Play of Hue in the Field of
Unknowing and Nebulosity

This Union is Your Breath and Breadth of Inspiration

Bridging All That Is

RSVP: Rebel Soul Venerated Presence

≈

The Bridge From Bondage to Bonding

As the reasons, seasons, and life times pass, all in the Universe changes into new forms. The new forms reflect the evolution of the times in which they are born. The history of your world and your individual way of being create the irresistible rush of the future. The rush is in anticipation of greater expression...but in that creative capacity, you cast another piece within the play. This is the ego. Just as everything outside of you is you, the you-niverse... everything inside of you is the you-niverse-city; an institution of higher learning. In moving through life experience, you graduate through many levels of understanding and awareness. The ego actually supports this process—guides it, in fact.

Ego is the governing head you chose as identity simply because it is your unique point of filtered perspective. The ego arose as a means of protection and service for the greater good, and helps manage the experience of other "heads of a state" that surround you. It intentionally has no ill will. Its prime directive was to give you a perspective to grow from. Ego creates the angst necessary to spike the deepest level of creation so to expand into greater being, or to pressure you into the deepest level of insecurity, so to be imprisoned by a smaller aspect of government. Our outer experience of government is a reflection of this. We are divided and insecure, at war and withholding, corrupt and desiring to self-correct. If you have a distaste for politicians, look at how you have been one, inside and out.

You were born to live in the land of the free. Understand, you are "bound" to be free.

Bondage is rooted deeply on the inside. It is in the unconscious and displays itself outwardly as chaos, challenge, obstacles, manipulation, and neediness. Dysfunction is a misaligned attempt to

create freedom, a self-organizing auto-correct. Can one free himself from any situation he is in? Force and will create a sense of getting loose, albeit a false sense of freedom, but bondage will remain
if the roots still exist.

We create challenge to provide a false sense of power. Obstacles
allow individuals to think they can figure out a way to control what
is going on, emerging victorious and free. But in reality, the unconscious programming is in control, providing a distraction, focus,
or project to work on, through, or out of. It is busy work, enslaving
us to a task rather than proceeding to our true purpose, which is
experience experiencing itself.

Immersion in chaos and challenge are self-created manifestations of boredom, restlessness, and frustration. Boredom engages
the flipside of creative capacity. This is the derelict side that wants
to escape by seeing action take place rather than being action. It is
an attempt "to experience" instead of fully emerging as experience.
You will know this, because it will be more mentally directed than
heart-fully lived. You will plot it, plan it, and contrive it. It will be
all thought out as the mind manipulates various outcomes. In other
words, the ego gets busy and makes up a story or fantasy, creating
"another life" of separation. This behavior creates bondage through
hiding, secrets, and lies. Each step into the story brings more ties
that bind, until there is no way to move. When immersed in such
a story or distortion, there are many choices. None of these will be
truly conscious choices and will involve a smaller group of individuals engaged in like thought, word, and action. Some examples
of the distorted behavior of illusion would display as gossip, addiction, embezzlement, or affairs. These experiences will be limited
to those select few people in collusion. Illusion is exclusive, where-
as true reality of aligned empowered and authentic expression is

inclusive. Reality and truth would always play out as communion, communication, compassion, fairness, and autonomy. When living out the reality of our highest expression, words, thoughts, and actions serve a greater good, allow for a sustaining ripple effect, and empower others through example and permission.

Restlessness is another form of unconscious distraction and is equally enslaving. It keeps an individual on the run. You are either moving from one thing to another, never fully engaging, or you are involved in too many things, never fully focusing. In either case, you are never at rest long enough to truly discover you are safe. Although you are not being chased, you run from feeling. You are not going to be caught, because you already are: caught in your own spin, going nowhere. The restless person may feel free because they constantly move from one thing to another, but they cannot escape. This busyness does not let them see they are heading right into the very depths they wish to avoid, swimming in the murky waters of their own making.

A feeling of restlessness courses within you and your life. This restlessness often stems from a sense of boredom. Despite the fact that you fill your days with endless tasks, people to take care of, and situations to manage, something is missing. Often times, your thoughts wander, questioning your life purpose. You may inquire as to how to create more meaning in your life, but then you shame yourself into realizing there is no real appreciation for what exists. If there were, there would be no need to seek out reasons to fill your time. Regardless of how you may want to deny this, statements you hold internally will be spoken in your presence. Our words and our actions speak volumes about what we believe to be our truth. Eventually the restlessness turns into frustration.

Frustration is a simmering anger that increases in intensity and heat until it has to boil over. However, boiling over does not create freedom; it simply lets it have the ability to recline back into the state of simmering. This is the ultimate bondage, because it is steeped in denial—denial of power, denial of importance, and denial of ability—all the while, complete denial of the self. Instead of expressing the self, outward projections provide the people and situations to keep the frustrations simmering at the core. If you are holding power but not wielding it, are "seeming important" but not standing in it, have ability but not utilizing it, know inherently you are free, but not letting yourself live in such a manner, you are in this state of bondage. Frustration can be described as desire to grasp something outside your self, but holding your own hands behind your back instead. It is the desire to move into something, but stopping your feet from stepping forward into it. It is being of full capacity, but having the weight of grievances and resentment, and the excuses that claim someone or something has taken your power, as a ball and chain that hold you in place. Frustration is self-imposed bondage.

Sometimes the deepest of these frustrations is knowing that gratitude should be held, but not feeling grateful at all. After all, you have this story, right? You were sent to this planet, planted in a family that was somewhere between somewhat ideal to radically dysfunctional. You were ingrained with the ideas "Life is hard. I have to protect myself. People hurt me. I cannot trust anyone. Karma will get me. God can get angry. I will be judged." And, yet, you are supposed to be positive, happy, and grateful? What is that about?

There is a belief that you have held, consciously or unconsciously, to try to change yourself so that you become more grateful. This is what everyone tells you as they speak, in an attempt to take their own advice. This is what you repeat to yourself, muttering it beneath your breath as a mantra, trying to etch it into every cell of your being, before someone finds out you are not really grateful: *"Be grateful for what you have. It could always be worse. Count your blessings."*

Will you be honest with yourself? Radically honest? If this is not your false truth, then your life will reflect it. But if it is, then you will have had reflections to prove it. We cannot be grateful until we acknowledge that we are not. We cannot fully allow and receive the situations that will create gratitude until we speak honestly to that false truth. Lack of gratitude requires the need to fill up with something, anything, everything.

Although a part of you knows you "should" be grateful, there is a desire for something more. When the well of gratitude is running dry, attempts to fill it come through a variety of means: a new pair of shoes, a sparkly new bauble, a great new piece of furniture, a grand trip, or a new car. But these drops in the well do not last very long. In fact, unbeknownst to you, they become symbols of how embedded you are in the life you live. They become the things that trap you into more of the existence you are living. You are bound to them and they are bound to you with invisible ties and tremendous weight. After a while, instead of gratitude for these things, they become tossed aside, as does your worth. Just as items lose value upon the shelf, the more things accumulated and not fully appreciated make you feel worth less as well. Slowly and steadily, you build a gilded prison of all things you wanted but did not need. Little do you know you are in bondage, each item a cord around your throat squeezing tighter, not allowing the scream that so desperately desires to be heard. These attachments become the reasons and justifications of why you must stay where you are: in the life you live but do not want. Whether you believe it or not, these accumulations do help you claim a false sense of gratitude as you say to others: "We are so fortunate to have so much. I am so blessed. We have been truly lucky."

But, the voice is flat, the eyes glaze over, and a longing sits in your heart. Understand these things are your escape, as are the statements that follow them. There is nothing wrong with material things. However, we are in the wrong when we identify with them as who we are or how we gauge others.

It was time to be honest with myself. Why had I stayed in this relationship for so long? There were multiple reasons to leave, but I had not. I always felt it was because I was afraid of the cultural letdown, the internal letdown, and what it would do to my children. Could I be radically honest with myself?

I stared around the room at all of the beautiful things we had. There were many, reminders of beauty I was attempting to create in my world. All these years, I could not let go of the safety, the security. I had stayed because I was afraid of the unknown, afraid of discovering I had no value or way to support myself. I had spent years creating valuable media resources but I had given them away! Why did I do that? Is it that I did not feel valuable enough to receive in exchange? Was it that I did not believe people would pay for them? Or was it that I really did not like the binding feeling of money because I had bound myself in this way to this marriage? What I knew in that moment is that I did not want any of it. None of it mattered anymore. I wanted to see a new world. Was that altruistic? Was I just ahead of my time? Was I simply a pioneer? Most would look at me and say, "Don't be crazy. You have a good life. You are comfortable. If you wanted to, you could sit back and never do a thing, buy whatever you want and have an easy ride."

But to me this life had no meaning. There was no intimacy and no connection. I was making my work my lover and filling days with tasks to pass the time. I was in bondage to my life, my marriage, my things, and soon my work, unless things changed. In letting go of what I had, I had nothing to lose and everything to gain. I was taking the chance to love me, to be courageous and committed to myself like I had never been before. It did not matter if other people understood it. I knew I just had another awakening.

What we really crave is not more stuff, but the inner experience of abundance and beauty. In this moment, you may be offended, believing that you are grateful, that you truly appreciate what you have, and that you have a sense of worth. If that is the case, why is there depression, sadness, or dis-ease? Why are you using affirmations or even reading this book?

There is nothing inherently wrong with material things when they are allowed to be pure experience. The distortion arises when there is craving and need, a belief that I am less than or wounded without these things. Why do you have the need to collect more, engage in excess, or prove your value through external gratification? What part of you are you trying to fill up? What are you really attempting to connect to?

The material world is not the only way you pursue fulfillment. Seeking out the adoration, acknowledgment, and approval of others keeps you settling into the comfort zones that fit the parameters of others' lives. By using them to fill you up, you choose to stay as small, standing in their shadow, which is why you often meet their shadow side. From the obviously codependent relationships to those that appear the most spiritual—where there is a belief in teacher and student, guru and guru-oupie, leader and follower—these attachments that you have are holding you tightly. As you stand behind them, following their lead, notice what you are bound to. You are enhancing their experience instead of empowering your own. You are in bondage to another's life and cannot be free to live your own.

You may ask, "If there are no teachers and students, no leaders and followers, what is to come of the world?" The answer: we would have a world of masterful beings creating to full capacity in their freedom. That can only result in abundance and a true display of power and presence. Belief in the need for a teacher or guru is only an affirmation of incompleteness. This is another pathological or path-of-logical thinking, and logical thinking got us where we are, so it is a bit overrated.

Notice how you are turned when following another; you are facing a back. Herein is the message: Turn toward yourself, to the you that thinks you are less than you are, less than you're worth. Lead and guide yourself. When you look down at your hands, you may discover you hold the ropes of your own hanging, your bondage, your enslavement. You need only create a new bond that leans toward your powerful truth, letting go of the ropes that bind you. In that moment, you will see that you have been "bound" for freedom all along.

It is within your attachments, in and to each passing season, that you become lost. In that space, the mystery is no longer a mystery but a maze, one in which you meander aimlessly, seeking to find the escape, yet longing for the center, your center. In actuality, the maze is you.

What is it that you wish to escape? Yourself, your beliefs, your limits, your life? You desire escape from the beautiful embellished prison you have created: your identity, your job, your relationships, your collection of things, and your pain. Yet, God forbid, you admit this to anyone, especially yourself! It becomes easier to wander aimlessly, creating all of the excuses and reasons, the ample justifications, why it must be as it is. And the greatest excuse is "I paid a lot for that." Yes, you did, and you might still be paying for it. Or you may say, "It cost me a lot. How can I let it go?" Yes, it has cost you a lot. Why would you hang onto it? These are the secrets you keep.

Yet, God knows your deepest secrets. The crumbling that occurs around you is the revealing of those hidden secrets. Your Beloved loves you enough to only give you what you truly desire, but even that desire has been tucked away in such a perfect hiding place. It has been so deftly hidden, you do not know where you have placed it.

Desires can only come in "perfect order," and that would also mean in the order in which they serve the greatest reward. That Divine Order may mean the tearing down of all structures that hinder the greatness of Self realization, of Divine Mastery. That order is an ordained path of divination. You are not to be in a maze, you are to experience "a-maze-meant" of the Highest order, into the center of the unknown, but up and out of the limited fantasies of the fragmented false self. Only the rebel can support the complete unveiling of this multi-dimensional experience.

Those who have not reached awareness of their bondage are also trapped by the desires they have. The desires they do not believe are possible are put on God. These are placed at God's feet, not always as a request, but often times as the small child, back turned, legs taut, arms crossed, and face pouting in sternness. The child demands, *"Over here! Show me God! Show me you love me! Show me I am worthy of this! Show me you are real and will give me what I ask for! If you don't, I know you do not really love me...and I will not believe in you! I will not trust in you!"*

Instead of being vulnerable and real by revealing these true fears, doubts, and desires for love, polite spiritual statements or apathetic throwaways are used, still pointed in God's direction as Divine responsibility: *"I will sit with it. If it is to be, it will be. It is up to God.... If it is God's will.... Let me pray on it. I will wait for it to be brought to me."*

Is this not spiritually embellished victim consciousness? Have you not placed yourself at the whim and fancy of a God that has the ability to punish, deny, and bully? If so, what is the nature of this Almighty force you base your life upon? You are already setting up a life of bondage and enslavement in having this type of relationship. You are engaging a separation of two, by claiming one strong and one weak. One as the controller and the other controlled—a master and a slave.

I get it; I understand. Often times, we pick these things up because we hear others say them, and it sounds spiritual. As I embarked upon the Rebel Road, something within me began changing. I began seeing how we use words and thoughts as a way to sidestep our authentic power.

Instead, why don't we commune with God, bond with this force that we are all a part of and that is a part of us? Why do we keep God at a distance, when that very presence is inside of us, is US? Why do we not realize that this magnanimous force has the capability and power to bring all things together? By simply coming through us, being within us, as us, we each have that same ability. We need only bond ourselves to thIS, to one another, which is more of thIS. The missing piece? Our own ability to unify with what we are! In this bond of unity, it is not possible to do anything other than attract, and receive, what is in the highest and best truth and expression of "Hue" we really are!

A very important piece has been abandoned here, and in doing so we have abandoned ourselves and have abandoned God-Source-Universe. What is it you think Source Presence wants? Why on Earth has He-She-It-All put you here? What other reason than to engage with you, to truly bond within you, to joyfully play with you, to Truth-fully, honestly create through you?

Step out of bondage and BOND—Being One Now Divine. Stop sitting in separateness and unify your Being! Stop standing in defiance and move into alliance! Quit pouting and start playing! Quit crying and begin creating! Quit stalling and begin moving! This is co-creation, not "God, go create!"

Unless you recognize how you engage the bondage experience, you will be challenged in creating clear, conscious choice. Expressions of restlessness, boredom, or frustration will cage the self. True freedom can never come from these types of expressions. You are either the slave or the master. You cannot be both. You cannot have a foot in two worlds. You are either out-of-line or aligned. You are either ONE or separate. Who are you? What are you choosing? What will you now have as your experience?

True freedom is the willingness to feel all things, in their fullness, allowing them to pass through. This would mean that no emotion is held or carried. It would also mean being conscious of being detached. Detachment is not a place of no-feeling or numbness. It is the state of allowing everything to be a part of you without the need to cling to it, make up stories, or hold memory or baggage. Detachment recognizes the Divinity, power, and strength in all things. It removes the need to save, fix or heal anything. Feelings are simply to be experienced, expressed, and dissolved into the Allness that you are. Feelings are the way humans attune experience and express sound. We are to synthesize the world, which means bring into oneness. Experiential integration increases the Light quotient and harmonizes wholeness for the cells. Freedom is the responsibility of creating choices that provide a benevolent Universe, one filled with the highest expression within both the inner world and the outer world.

The only one that truly controls the degree of freedom you have is you. The degree to which you free yourself and express the essence of freedom is the degree to which your world will reflect that back at you. You are the journey. In order to be totally free, you need only develop awareness and action. Freedom can never be destroyed, but it can be given away. Freedom is not "being able to do what you want." Freedom is recognizing the responsibility for creating the benevolent world that you most desire.

The inherent essence of freedom requires of us only one thing: to BOND. Your freedom lies within your ability to bond to all that is outside without strings of attachment, all that is inside without being weighted down by it, all that is Divine about you without believing that experiences of bondage are required to earn your way there. You are already ALL THAT. You need only to *BOND* with it. *Being One Now Divine*. Who could you be, if you let yourself have full freedom? Who could others be, if you let them have their freedom? What would this world look like if each person lived in the consciousness of freedom? What would we create through strengthening our BOND?

YOU ARE INVITED TO

UNION AND COMMUNION WITHIN

ALL SPACES AND TIMES,

EVERYWHERE KNOWN AND UNKNOWN,

MULTIPLE REALMS AND DIMENSIONS

ALLOWING AND ENGAGING

MIND—BODY—SPIRIT—EGO—SELF

BEING ONE NOW DIVINE

I AM THAT I AM

RSVP: RIGHTING SELF'S VIRTUE-ALL PERCEPTION

The Bridge From Servitude to Service

You may be in very churning times and situations in your experience. You may simply desire something more out of life—out of your self? Forces are flowing together and breaking apart "your" world as you have come to know it. In order to create a new experience, it must be churned with willingness and attention, in a container of Divine Knowing. You are the milk that has been squeezed from the Divine, now being churned or agitated to make butter, still as much the sacred and holy Essence, just another expression of the Divine. And then, you shall reinvent yourself as some other transformation of the butter. This is the play of the Divine in its infinite possibility, its ever-expanding creation to know the vastness of itself. Each step is in service to the next. Each incarnation serves the Divine in experience. Each reinvention is an act of union with power and possibility.

In many ways, you will be the example for others in the days ahead, but you are not yet fully understood, especially to yourself. You may even be mistrusted, or the center of interpersonal up-heaval. But all the stress and strain you are currently experiencing is strengthening you for the changes that must come. This isn't a time for facades, pretentious talk, and ego-mania. Such behavior will reveal the confusion and insecurity that keeps you in servi-tude. In this moment, you may discover your servitude is to what you have always done—or shall I say the beliefs, patterns, behaviors, and mannerisms you have engaged with.

Have you searched out the quick fix? Do you desire a methodol-ogy, technique, affirmation, or healing that would rapidly change things? Have you been running after a teacher, guru, or someone who is seemingly above others? Is this how you have been bypass-ing your life? Yes, bypassing. To a certain degree, all of these things are a means of distraction. It may feel like it is about you, but it has just enough entertainment that your mind will easily create an-other point of focus. We are deceptively cunning when it comes to escapism. If you are trying to find a means of escape from where you are, then you are not experiencing what you are in, which only keeps it locked in place.

This is one way you give away your gift of experience, handing your precious divine power to another. The fallback tools you are taught, used at a surface level without truly integrating you in the experience of them, keep you strung along like a puppy. Don't you know teachers provide techniques they gain through experience, their experience? It is what worked in their lives. What makes you think it will work in yours? You are unique. You will discover your own truth. Why wear another's? When you follow them in this way, placing them on a pedestal higher than yourself, you give them your power.

They have access to your power and their own grows because of it. You are in servitude to them and do not even know it. Can you honor their journey, acknowledge their path, take from it what you need, and be on your way as your own journey? If you have become a guru-oupie, you are not really present to the journey that you are. Rather, you are present in the journey that they are.

So you ask, "But, if I do not follow someone who knows what I do not, how will I grow?" You believe, "I am wounded and broken. They are in their purpose and power. They know something I do not. They have something I do not." You think, "Let me say these affirmations, light this candle, burn this incense. Let me set the sacred space, put up an altar, figure out the exact music to play, and sit in the position that appears correct. Let me remember to breathe the way this one told me to, focus on the place that one said was important, and chant the mantra that those people did." You surmise, "If I wear white, place crystals on my body, smudge myself, and throw salt in the corners, grace may fall upon me." And then you say, "I do not know how to do this. Let me attend another workshop, gain another certification, learn another technique, read another 10 books, listen to some more inspirational talks, and find some positive images to post on Facebook." All the while, you feel exhausted and no more enlightened than before, especially when the next boulder hits.

I say all of this not to condemn any of these things or to say these teachers have nothing to offer. I am certainly not telling you that these things are a waste or wrong. There will be things you can gain or learn. I am pointing out that your intention may be the problem. All of the statements above are descriptions of being in servitude, an illustration of being in servitude to ritual and to the teacher that taught it. You have made it into dogma. These encompass doing something for an end result, not for the sake of "being experience." This is no different than robotically and numbly playing follow-the-leader.

Can you stop long enough to figure out what feels right to you, what may be sacred to you? It does not have to look like what everyone else does; it likely will not. In fact, what is unique to you is what will work for you. When you engage in this way, your journey becomes about the experience of you in the moment, not a rush to the finish line or an attempt to acquire something that is missing or lacking. Repetitive doing is going to result in servitude if you are trying to gain an outcome with the sole intention of getting out of where you currently are.

How do you move this from servitude to service? Rather than the intention being escapism-based, allow the attention to be anchored in full-sensory immersion of experience. Allow the intention to create the space for fully realizing and knowing the experience of the situation that you are currently in and your creation within it. Let your intent always open your experience to the Mastery of you, which in many moments will appear as you not knowing what step to take but being willing to take one. It is easy to be an individual who walks among miracles, but a Master is not surrounded by miracles. A Master knows how to walk through anything; they are willing to walk through everything. Be in service to your Mastery, instead of in servitude to false masters. These are false idols.

The ego wants to be credentialed, certified, finish a program, earn a status. Just be open to experiencing another or their work for as long as it feels appropriate. You will always be led to what you need. You will always find yourself in front of the one that has a piece of your puzzle, but it does not mean you must stay there. When the moment arises where you feel complete, move on. Do not let the ego, or society's unconscious bullying, demand you follow through something if you authentically feel it is time to stop.

Are you utilizing intention or in-tension? Doing creates tension. It also engages the deep-seated sense of restlessness, boredom, and frustration that creates bondage. Servitude is a precursor to bondage.

Unlike doing, being utilizes intention as a sacred container for divine creation to take place. Let focused intention be the birthing ground of expansion and infinite possibility. When engaging in any undertaking—problem, illness, the challenge of a new project, job, or experience—change your intention first in your phrasing or approach. Instead of:

- *"How do I get out of this?"* ask *"How do I dive fully into this?"*
- *"How do I stop this?"* ask *"How do I start something new within this?"*
- *"How do I heal this?"* ask *"How do I embrace this fully?"*
- *"How do I fix this?"* ask *"How do I build something from here?"*
- *"How do I save them from where they are?"* ask *"How can I savor where they are?"*

The questions on the left are from a space of identifying with the other person or a situation. The new questions on the right have a different energy and intent. Rather than servitude, they bring in the energy of service. They open the space for you to experience yourself in new ways. They have the energy of allowance, inviting creative capacity to flow in. In addition, they support a sense of connection rather than fueling more separation. This is service to the Self, which ultimately becomes service to the other, the ONE.

In going back to discover what you don't know, and the many things that you do know, experience in service is quite different from that of servitude. There is a misconception regarding service. Most people think it is about serving others, those people and things on the outside. Charity begins at home. Be in service to yourself first. Be in service to your body, your health, and your well-being. Be in service to your dreams, desires, and creativity. Be in service to your voice and needs. Service is open-hearted and expansive. Because you are filling yourself up through the exchange of the experience, you are gaining connection, love, and Self.

Servitude will always have an undercurrent of conscious or unconscious resentment. This position will make an individual feel tired, used, and depleted. The world will begin to feel abusive and ungrateful. For example, imagine two individuals in the political field at the same level, for the same period of time. One refers to himself as a public servant. The other says that she is engaged in public service. These may not appear radically different, but they invite and initiate a completely different set of situations and experiences. A public servant will often have thoughts that he will never be able to please the public, and will create situations to prove that. The politician that refers to public service views herself as a part of the very public she serves. One will leave politics early; the other will have a lifelong career. Can you see which it would be?

But, how do you learn what you do not know? Maybe *that* is a story. Make it up. Make it up as you go along. You were creative enough to make up all kinds of other stories that got you where you are. There have been so many times where you have created entire conversations between other people, and you were not even present. There have been moments when you decided where someone might have gone, who might be planning against you, or how a scenario is going to go down. You are creative enough to make all kinds of things up...and believe them to be true!

Consider how powerful tsunamis or hurricanes are, the kind of intensity they possess. Imagine how things are cleared out, swept away, or spun around. Are you currently in or have you been in chaos or a crisis? Liken that to a tsunami or a hurricane in your life. You created that tsunami experience in your life. You must be something powerful to have brought up that kind of storm. If you are powerful enough to create hurricanes and tsunamis in your world, can you imagine the power and presence you truly possess and all that you actually can create? Weather the storms that are present. As you move through them, make up a great new story, a creative, power-filled one.

Do not go out to follow a teacher or speaker because you think they have the answers to solve your problems. Go to them because you want to experience you in that setting. You want to experience them as you. They appear as a mirror to you. Go because you desire an experience of connection, community, engaging, and learning with yourself. Let this be a place of expansion. Breathe it in, hold sacredly the moment, and when you leave, breathe it out. Allow the experience to have a beginning, middle, and end. Then, move into your next experience. They have appeared before you to give you one thing—not a lesson, not a teaching, not a method or a ritual; they are here to give you a glimpse of your power. In service to that, to yourself, to the need that directed you to them in the first place, allow the inner creative essence to be your teacher, guru, and guide. Your soul did not guide you there to be led. Your soul led you there as your guide. Do not project that power onto someone else; it belongs to you.

How do you learn the way through life experiences? You live through them. You begin in service to them, desiring to be that. You proceed in service to them, wondering what they look like on you. You engage in service with them, as you teach what you need to learn. You serve by discovering new ways to reinvent who you are. By virtue of experience, you embody a new way of being and become the very thing you were once enamored by.

You may believe that all those others—the healers, authors, teachers, gurus, coaches, speakers—have something you do not. You may think they have no obstacles. Their only difference is how they use their creative capacity to experience themselves teaching what they need to learn. Don't you know they truly are only speaking to themselves? They have been just as broken and wounded at times, but they use challenge as a place to begin, rather than it bringing them to their end. They are Masters because they create what they desire to experience themselves as, despite their obstacles, challenges, and hiccups. They have nothing you do not. They simply chose to be "in action" instead of maintaining "inaction."

What happens to you in your life does not stop you; you stop you. When you do, you are in servitude to what has happened. You are in servitude to the challenge and the chaos. Instead, be in service to what can happen through you. Teach yourself what you need to learn by talking about, creating, and living it.

When you say affirmations, pray, or meditate, do not perform a ritual. Do not do it to fix or save someone or something. When you do so, you actually keep the person or situation in place. Your doing will have no energy in it, because your being is not really in it. Affirmations, prayer, meditation, movement, breath work, chanting—anything, everything—is only effective and valuable if you are engaged in the experience of yourself within it, for the primary purpose of experience experiencing itself.

Are you in your heart or in your head? If you are following steps, you are in your head. If you are wondering why or wandering, you are not present. Lose yourself to the moment and immerse yourself fully into the experience of it—mind, body, spirit, heart, and soul. Let it be full sensory—taste, touch, smell, sight, sound—intuitive and with lightness. The same is true for anything, from lighting a candle and playing music, to getting dressed and having a night on the town. Everything is spiritual. Taking out the garbage, washing the dishes, changing a diaper, mowing the grass... even the mundane is steeped in the spiritual. It is spiritual because the experience exists, and because you are in creation with it. The fullness of spirit is present when you are engaged to it, married to it, in union with it. All is spiritual, everything from home, family, and practice, to jobs, recreation, and dysfunction, but only when your Spirit is in it.

Even a post on social media should represent the full-bodied expression of you, for no one else but you. It should not matter if anyone else reads it, comments on it, agrees with it, or believes it to be valuable. It is not about how many things you can post. Nor is it about having something to do because you are bored. Make sure you are fully present with it, and then it truly serves. When you are that intimately engaged in every experience, servitude cannot exist because you are in complete service to yourself. And if everything that exists is ultimately YOU in disguise, all will be served.

This is a time for looking at the world with a clear and disciplined eye. It is an opportunity for personal dedication. All the signs point to transformation for you, the Mastery of you. First, feelings about changes that need to be made will well up. You will sense that pieces and parts of you will desire to be present or "be the present." As the structures that have defined you begin to disassemble, your decision to dive into the unknown of yourself will emerge. This is the space where the small self can be given back unto the Divine Self, allowing it to lead and guide in the place of its truth, absolute expression, presence, and creativity. A new you will begin to surface as the old you stands back in wonder.

For this to happen, an engagement must occur. It is the step into love, courage, and commitment that forges a marriage of the trinity: the small self, the Higher Self, and the True All-knowing Divine Self. Your outer appearance or demeanor, and your inner attitude or philosophy, must evolve to align with and embody the rising soul of the new days in which you find yourself. These days will feel similar to the past but be uniquely different. No matter what has held you back before, you will feel compelled to rise beyond it. You will deeply feel that your greater risk lies in remaining who you have always been, rather than diving into the unknown you have yet to discover. There may not yet be words to describe what is to be done or how, there is only a knowing to go where you have never gone before.

You will make the choice to be courageous in the face of fear, leading by example. Others will know you by your walk, deeds, and integrity. Within the churning, you will see the Light that you choose to stand in has been the Light of all creation. The only difference is that you no longer reach for the Light as something outside of you. Rather, you embody the Light as what has always been you. Instead of standing in the shadows of Light, identifying with the darkness and believing you stood behind something greater than yourself, you now live as Light, owning your Divinity and knowing you are the brilliance that casts light, shadow, and everything that is illuminated and hidden within that play of creation.

You are the weather of the seasons. You will succeed because you are not witnessing creation, you are creation. You are not witness to a play, you are the play. You are not here to do anything in the world; you are the world and everything in it. Receive in every moment and when you do so, you are in celebration. It's all you, right now. It is *all* you.

The Universe has been having a conversation with you all along. You may have paid attention; you may have not. Nonetheless, the conversation has been constant. Many mirrors have been placed in front of you to enhance your experience of you. In fact, all that you see in the outside world is you, every piece and part a symbol of you created to play with you. There is no one here but YOU.

Every person, experience, and circumstance is a reflection of you. It may not be a reflection you are aware of. That is why it appears. These parts of you are to be brought to awareness. There are no accidents, coincidences, or random happenings. Everything is in sync with who you are internally, in that moment. All of your experiences and the people with whom you engage are you in a different form to bring back parts unto yourself. They appear different than you, but what if it is all you? Everything. There is no one in the room but YOU.

As you assemble the awareness of these fragments and identify where they are lodged, you move closer to the land of "unknowing."

When you embrace all that exists outside of
you as the rest of you...

When you love what is outside of
you as if it exists inside of you...

When you allow the ugliness and pain outside of
you to fully express inside of you...

When you bear witness to the beauty surrounding
you and know it as you...

You will be able to fully engage and integrate wholeness.

The moment is present to wed to the
All-ness and truth of you...

To immerse yourself as Divinity expressing
in, as, through, and around you.

Forget about mind, body and spirit; this too is separation.

Life is your union and communion, the marriage
of reality and illusion.

So, here it is: there is only one of us here. It is you. Secondly, the you that you see is not the body, not the mind that you identify with, not your personality, not your education, marital status, or bank balance. The body is the spacesuit you travel in. The mind is the computer system by which you navigate. You are beyond these things. This may be hard for you to fathom, yet a part of you is contemplating the vastness of this, the vastness of you. If you are not the body or the mind, what are you? If you are not all of what you have believed yourself to be, then who are you? What are you? Where are you?

You are experience experiencing itself. You are all experience. You are all conversation. In fact, everything that appears in your world is the experience of YOU, as that conversation. Why are you only seeing from your identity's perspective? It is because you have limited your perception into that narrow arena of focus.

Who would I be now? As I pondered completely letting go of the identity I had held for 18 years of my marriage, I saw what my life had been. Who could I be if I let go of all the beliefs I had about myself? What could I experience if I were not in servitude to the personality, identity, and expression I had experienced myself as?

I knew what it meant to be a doer...a worker...a workaholic. I knew how to be isolated, a hermit and an introvert. I knew how to be disciplined and focused. I knew how to work alone and not have a team of support. It was clear I was quite adept at loving, giving, and serving.

What was my unknown? What did I want to experience myself as? Even if I did not know how, what was I willing to at least invite into my experience. This tension I was feeling was the degree of servitude I was in to all of these known parts of me. In this moment, both service and freedom rested on stepping into unknown parts of me.

As usual, I spoke aloud, "Okay, here it is. I am ready for friends, real friends...good, strong, true connections. I desire a circle of women I can engage with, women who have done their work, who are not intimidated and who know how to be real and vulnerable. I desire to get out and experience life, experience myself in life in all kinds of new experiences. Rather than disciplined and focused, I open to an organic unfolding and self-organizing structure. I want to laugh, dance, sing, and play. I want to play and have fun. I want to lighten up."

It felt scary. This truly was unknown, but I also felt the resurgence of aliveness! For many, this may seem frivolous, but it was my unknown. Does this world exist within me? Does this world exist around me? I am willing to discover it. How could I move beyond my self?

Imagine that you have a straw that you peer through. With that "tunnel" vision, you will focus on one image, whatever fits within the circle of the straw. But you are not the straw. You are not even the eye peering through the straw, nor the thoughts that cross while gazing at the object within the perception. Yet, you believe that is the entire world during the experience of it. In fact, you believe you are that.

However, if you stepped back from the straw, you may discover there is a lot more than you let yourself see. You will also discover that you are more than what your eye, mind, or perspective held. If you were to expand your attention to encompass broadened awareness, you would become witness of more than you see and experience now. There are moments when you already venture there. Eventually, you will see you are more than what you see and experience now.

When you walk into a room and feel something in the air, it is you all over the place in awareness. Déjà vu experiences are you in all space and time, rather than a one-sense perception. Dreams also portray a broader expanse of experience. Knowing who is on the other end of the phone, or sensing something before it happens, illustrates situation where you are expanding perception. In the moment you choose to recognize you as everything, the puzzle pieces of you come together and become one complete picture. That is when you will uncover the face of the unknown.

As of now, you have only allowed yourself to see some of the masks that are covering your true face. Although you were the one that placed them there, you have not been able to see them. There are many kinds of masks; they encompass physical limitations, emotional wounding, attachments, and identification with certain experiences. The masks can also be your passions, social status, economic status, career, degree, and ethnicity. Anything you become so identified with that it becomes who you are and how you move is one of your masks. This is the limited perception of your truth.

When your focus and your life are entrenched in things such as these, your thoughts, actions, and motives will be based on upholding them. Rather than serving you on your journey as accessories to your experience, you end up in servitude to them as the only experience.

Carolyn suffered a terrible car accident when she was 31 years old. A drunk driver hit her head on, completely changing her life. After many months in the hospital and multiple surgeries for a broken back, she was told she would never walk again. Yet her will and belief were strong. She was determined to walk again, and she did. Ten years later, she was off of ninety percent of her medications and walking on both legs without assistance of any support mechanisms. What she had accomplished was a miracle of the mind, body, and spirit. Yet, so often invitations would arise for various experiences and her reply would be, "I am limited by my physicality."

Despite being a miracle walking, her journey through paralysis was still present in how she allowed it to stop her from fully participating in life. She was in servitude to her old beliefs of her body, rather than being in service to the living miracle that she is. The truth was that she had already transcended the limitations of her physicality by walking again and coming off her medication. A powerful mind and spirit that was able to will her to walk again also created statements of lack, negativity, or limitation that were equally powerful. Her servitude to the idea of having physical limitations and paralysis had become more important than being in service to the part of her that truly wanted to live. Her condition had been her focus, project, and goal for so long that she did not know how to live without it. Even though the paralysis and limitation had been willing to leave her, she was not willing to leave it.

In every life, there are the moments when we find ourselves in the void. This is a place of nothingness and nowhere. It has no direction and feels like a black hole. You know there is further to go, but don't have any idea how to get there. During these times, an individual has to let go, because there is nothing to cling to. None of the material means anything. This is a state of emptiness and vulnerability; it may feel as if you are enslaved by the conditions around you. Thoughts of failure, sadness, and loss of what could have been surround you. Here is where you might sink into disappointment. This is the moment you can fall deeper into servitude.

Disappointed means you have cast yourself down and received a lower standing than what your Truth Self knows you to be. The human part of you judges it and despairs. The Hue-man part waits now to "appoint" you back to your high standing. You are at a moment of choice: either you can take the lower standing and sink into greater servitude of where you are, or you can rise into this higher standing and be in service to that magnificence.

When in service, you have the ability to touch many. When in servitude, you barely can help yourself. Servitude confines you to living half-heartedly. You are not fully present. Your heart is not in it. More situations arise which will take you farther into feeling obligated and indebted to others, because you have not fully committed to yourself. You have projected that commitment onto other projects or other people. All the while, you live in longing for what you feel you have lost.

Service is a fulfilled state of being. You can be in gratitude for all you have to give. Service also stands in a "void," devoid of any sense of self so that it expands into the consciousness of "living as all." Service is living through the lens of auspiciousness and harmony. Auspiciousness is the feeling of abundance and beauty. It taps into a feeling of satisfaction and a sense of having enough, being enough. It is an inner feeling where nothing on the outside is required or needs to be fixed, because there is knowledge of inner harmony.

Harmony is composed of "Har" and "mony." In the eastern religions, Egyptian and Norse mythology, "Har" is considered the name of God. It is also known as the highest mountain. "Mony" pertains to expressing the attributes or qualities of. Harmony is the state we step into when in service. It is naturally awakened because this is inherent within us. When in harmony and service, there is no feeling of separateness. Our intent is to connect and be one with the other in empathy and compassion. As human beings, we naturally move toward states of harmony out of a deep desire to be of great service. Harmony can spontaneously occur or be developed as a habit, birthed within the adoration of being free and holding space for community and cooperation.

All humans have conditions that they are in servitude to. As long as man believes in a God outside of himself and deals with that Mighty Presence in a codependent manner, the human condition will remain. Human suffering depends on the existence of a separate authority, one that is higher and stronger than us, and with the power to punish us. Harmony is the God state within, pouring outward. Hue-man is the man illuminated with the Light of God. The heart in each one of us is the heart of God. Why would we put the Divine in servitude to anything less than the highest expressions of creativity, beauty, and goodness? Why would we deny God's expression in, as, and through us fully, by being in servitude to thoughts, ideas, beliefs, and actions that belittle this presence in our lives, in each one of us? Rather than turning outward in servitude, can there be a turning inward—actually a tuning inward—in service to the great ONE that only desires to experience and express beauty, love, and creation, allowing that knowing to be integrated completely as an experience.

Servitude does not only relegate itself to areas where there is weakness, dysfunction, or wounding. It can arise from passion and creation as well. Often, bouts of inspiration have us embark on creating powerful businesses, visions, causes, and manifestations. In joy, manifestations come into form. Excitement spurs these creations into full bloom, perhaps becoming immensely successful. Passion can also appear as organizations and communities you align with. While in the state of joy, celebration, inspiration, and creation, these too are "beings" in service while we are in service to them. Being in service expands the heart, connection, community, and expression. Every experience has a cycle that will birth, grow, and ask for completion. Creations are like a child whose presence dictates the course of life. It will define schedules and time, create obligations and needs. It will ask for nurturing, but eventually will control you. This original birthing has grown from the infant that has been wooed over and cared for lovingly, to becoming the demanding teenager that wants its own way, to the young adult that desires independence. What ensues is a power struggle that has the original creator of this entity pinned down. There can, and typically will, come moments when "the creation" takes over and becomes the false and controlling "God." All of a sudden, what was once a source of excitement becomes a place of obligation. That is the fine line between service and servitude. Service lets go; servitude holds on tight.

The moment you have slipped from the place of joy and celebration, experience and expression, you become enslaved by the very thing you created. It is not only limited to products, businesses, organizations, and causes. It can take the shape of relationship as well: spouses, partners, family, children, and parents. Servitude is any codependent experience that leaves you depleted and half-hearted. This is a moment where change is required. Either it has to change, or you have to change. In some cases, either it has to go, or you do. You can only save it and yourself by moving back into a place of joy and inspiration, either with it or away from it. Re-appointing yourself as the divine creator of your design engages the ease of letting go. The alternate solution is to birth a new vision, which may encompass a new creation and/or a new you.

Have you noticed that the Almighty Presence never gets emotionally attached to this earthly creation? The Divine is a very neutral force, desiring to play with every whimsy and desire requested. Regardless of whether thoughts and feelings are positive or negative, Creation grants that desire, with no attachment to the outcome. The Divine is in play with us...in complete celebration of the unfolding, fully present. God does not try to save us and is definitely not in servitude to us, no matter what our cries or demands may be. Why is that? The Divine knows its Truth, the Truth that flows in and through entire creation, a Truth so strong that it is to be celebrated into its revealing.

What if you lived your life in complete celebration and aliveness of every moment? What if you allowed every choice to be based on how it served you so that it could flow out as expanded service from your nourished full heart and being? What if you could view all of your creations—children, dreams, relationships, careers, interactions—as whole and Holy, knowing they possess the same power and presence to be, do, and have anything they desire, if willing to step into the light of their own magnificence? They are further pieces and parts of you, after all.

What if each day were a new day with nothing carried forward from the past, and nothing aimed into the future, so that there were no binding ropes in either direction? What if you lived as close to each moment as each inhale and exhale, only acting upon what the breath of that moment asked for?

What if there were no yesterdays or tomorrows, only the experience of this moment—Right Now. Yes, make this moment "right" now. Can you be in service to what this second is asking for you—not of you, but for you? Are you having a moment? Or, are you letting it pass you by? This is the moment! This is your moment! Today is Moment-Us!

~

You are Invited to the Dance of Beautiful Harmony in

Selfless Emanation Reflecting Vital Intimate

Committed Expression

Bridging and Being

Wonder Full

Timeless, Boundless, Formless Design

Into Consciousness Creating

Form—Heart—Voice—Energy—Action

Playing in the Light of Aliveness

I AM That I AM

RSVP: Reveal Service Visibly Present

~

The Bridge From Armor to Amour

The desire of all human beings is to love and be loved. In actuality, the greatest desire is to experience unconditional Love and the feeling of being completely cherished. Each person has been unconsciously seeking the honoring that celebrates who we are, regardless of what we do. The obstacle until now is how we "do" love. This comes from a perspective that we are outside of love and have to find a way into an experience of it. This is another thing we place on a pedestal, away or at a distance instead of realizing we are that.

It comes from the emotional conditioning and teaching that love exists as the actions of one human being to another, rather than the field that is able to hold the space for any and all action, response, and stillness. We have been so immersed in the field of Love that it has been invisible to us. How often have you said:

- Give me some love.
- Do you love me?
- I do love you.
- Can I have some love?

It is almost as if it needs to be bottled and served, prepackaged and handed over. We even created holidays around it to make it measurable. When tragedy strikes, we want to send people love, as if it left them, instead of realizing we need to see them in the field of love, as love. Love just is. It cannot be seen, measured, manipulated, harnessed, lost, or done. It can only be felt and known. Love is the frequency of all matter; our perceptions and separation dilutes that frequency.

As humans, because we are taught to do love and that it can be rationed, it is guarded. Through generations of wounded upbringing—not truly ever having learned what love is, how it is, or the magnitude of meaning—life experiences have been approached wearing armor. With the heart on guard, a human being cannot fully trust and, in kind, cannot be trusted. "On guard" means to be in defense of. The armor keeps away what is most desired, but also acts like a magnet to what is least wanted as experience. In attracting the challenges and pain that we try to protect ourselves from, we further guard ourselves, building up the layers of armor. This becomes an endless cycle of separation and disconnection, resulting in deepening the human condition. Just as an onion has layers and separations, the thin filmy skin is the armor—thin but strong veils that cannot be seen.

This would seem a fragile armor, flimsy, see through. But it is in this type of fragility that we hold the self tautly, not wanting to display any transparency. The thin skin of the onion is the thin skin of the false selves built upon one another. This is why we have easily crumbled in the past, in the hidden layers of shadows that have been the stories of our lives. If we just shed the skin of our paper-thin selves, like a snake, the armor that was worn can rub away. What we do not recognize is that the "rub" of life is love as well. Life can only love us because it is the field we live, work, and play in. The challenges and obstacles that appear are the experiences in love, of love, and with love for the self to bring us back to the frequency we truly are. Love always desires to attune us back into the oneness: amour instead of armor.

Love has also been a means of currency and exchange. This codependent behavior is used everywhere from relationships of intimacy to that of business and public matters. The fear of not being loved or the belief that our love has to appear a certain way has kept humans living small and afraid to fully express their unique natures. In fact, love is used to barter for the very things we do not want. Whether spouses, partners, or work dynamics, the distortions of love can play out many ways.

For example, in the traditional scenario, a woman marries a man because she wants to escape the restrictions, limitations, and expressions of love in her original family. Her unspoken barter is *"I will take care of you, support you and stand by you if you provide what I desire. Fill my life with excitement and pleasure, gifts and glory. Be my knight in shining 'armor' and take me from this place."* The man's unspoken barter is *"I will give you whatever you want if you take care of the home, handle the mundane, let me have my freedom, provide the sexual release, and let me do as I want. Let me be king. I desire someone to take care of me when I want it, in the way I want."* They marry and initially are happy because surface desires are met.

The woman finds herself caring for the home, the children, and the mundane tasks, and providing the social and sexual release. Soon, the material things are not enough. She wants time, connection, and communication. The man is usually not at home, and when he is home, he wants to take it easy. He feels he has worked hard, provided everything that was asked and deserves space. He is tired of talking, because he had to deal with people all day and does not understand how she does not understand that.

The woman becomes resentful. She really desires connection and her own sense of creativity and purpose, but she has been confined to a role that does not allow her to step beyond its parameters. The home, time spent alone, or building the nest becomes a prison. Her body becomes a machine to be used and her spirit a worn garment.

Meanwhile, the man also seethes because he grows weary of always doing and supporting, being the main breadwinner. He views the other as having a pampered, spoiled lifestyle, while he slaves away. This causes him to want to stay away from the home and have other outlets and escape. He too feels used, but also entitled.

Now, of course this is a generalization meant to illustrate that we have unspoken agreements, but I have seen this one in many clients' marriages.

If you want to know how something is going to end, watch how it begins. Everything has to come full circle. We are cycles, wheels within wheels. This woman came into this marriage as a means of escape. She was seeking freedom from where she was, so of course the situation coming full circle would mean she would need to re-experience the feeling of needing to escape. The man desired someone who would do everything for him, but that person would not be able to be everything for him. His commitment to providing was creating a machine that was burning out and becoming numb. The desire to be free remained as he found himself more imprisoned than ever.

The beauty of this is that no love has been lost. What they identified as love was never love at all. It was a barter transaction. The field of love brings everything full circle so that it may reproduce the same circumstances to let the individuals face their distortions of love, to let down their armor, to discover the unspoken false self which really said, *"Save me...fill me up...take care of me because...I am in danger...I am lacking...I am broken."* You may question this, but if you are in a relationship that feels like a rub, there are some unspoken agreements that are founded in disempowered, unloving, unspoken affirmations. Love does not know you as this and will not allow it to remain. Two unlike frequencies cannot exist in the same space. You are in and surrounded by love at all times.

Anything unlike love cannot remain. And LOVE knows you well enough to bring up anything unlike itself. You cannot escape your self or your Self. You must understand, you cannot "do" love. Love is "being" all the time. YOU are that being. Why would you think anything else? Why do you allow anything else? How does it serve you to distort love? Are you so afraid of your power that you would deny the very existence of it in your life? Or have you been so wounded, imprinted, and now completely enamored by betrayal that you would rather take fear to bed?

In this moment, you likely have read that statement a couple of times and have your head cocked to the side, thinking, *"I am not enamored with betrayal. I certainly do not take fear to bed."* Are you sure? Fear plagues most people today, and it is the greatest armor we carry. Fear is the mistress of the soul. It is your lover. It courts you and creates all kinds of feelings inside. Fear takes you dancing often, twirling you back and forth between the "what was" and the "what if." And just before you fall out of its arms, it grabs hold, pulling you close. Fear desires to keep you hidden. It will isolate you, not desiring to share you. It sees no need to celebrate you, because you give it all that it wants. Whispering all of the "nothings" to you—*you are nothing, you will have nothing, it will result in nothing*—you are entranced by its seeming power. Each and every time fear comes close, to whisper those sweet nothings, you feel quivering inside. It knows what to bring you. It always comes bearing the same gifts. And although you may not desire those gifts, you have gotten used to them. There is some kind of safety in them, in the knowing of them. But I must tell you that fear will eventually leave you. It is always seeking more lovers, never satisfied, and desires to take control of all. If it cannot have you, it will seek out others.

Your body shakes, your heart beats, any and every thought passes through your mind. You want to scream, shout, cry, laugh, stand up, and fall to your knees. This is because you feel the armor. You feel that which binds and guards you as a restriction. All of those sensations are Love coaxing you out and offering you something unconditional.

Steven carried within himself resentment and animosity. Once again, another relationship had fallen apart. How did this happen? What was worse, he had confided with a set of friends during the course of his pain and now those friends had distanced from him and united with his ex. Steven could not understand how he continually was betrayed. Along with his inability to fully forgive, he now had his guard up. As an individual who believed in inner work, he became frustrated that he could not resolve this one area of his life.

As we spoke, it was very evident he had formed armor around his heart. However, something in his language told me that even despite the armor, love still existed and he was using that love as a weapon against himself.

Steven proceeded to tell me how he and Candace had really loved each other, but she had come from a history of abandonment and would not deal with her issues (first clue...mirror, mirror). He also mentioned how he kept trying to help her, but the relationship evolved into her not desiring help, and his own temper flaring. They reached the point of no longer being kind to each other, and Steven decided the best thing was to leave.

I tried to assist him in realizing she had created the very same pattern she was afraid of, as had he. He continued to speak on and on about how creative she was.

His issue was not with her; it was with the two friends. He said all of his anger stemmed from their betrayal. When I asked him to go deeper into why he kept speaking of Candace so lovingly and yet could not do that for the friends, he replied, "I have had many relationships that have ended in this way. I truly loved her. I did everything I could to help her. It was just a relationship where I was less and less in my power because I was so focused on her. I want this to end in love. She has given me a lot of beautiful things." The next thing I knew he was describing piece after piece that she had made and given to him as gifts, including an art piece he had bought from her when they first met. I asked him why he still had those things.

"Why don't you get rid of them if the relationship is over? That seems painful to keep memories around when there is obvious turmoil. You are torturing yourself."

"But these are beautiful pieces made with love. I don't want to just throw them away. With every other relationship, I just got rid of everything and closed the door, never looking back. I wanted this to be different, so I am determined to keep these things and love her despite what has happened."

There it was: the bonding had turned into bondage. "Steven, if you had a painful splinter in your finger, would you leave it there?"

"No. I would remove it."

"If a knife cut your hand, would you keep the knife in your hand?

"No."

"Well, that is what you are doing with all of these objects. They are splinters and daggers in you. You use them to keep you in the relationship. You use them as weapons against yourself, and against Candace and your friends. As long as you have them around, they are your unconscious reminders."

"But I wanted to do this differently. I had to prove to myself I did not have to get rid of things and close the door."

"But you have never closed the door; you have only put them in the closet. All those past relationships still exist, and I know that because you created the exact same thing in this one. You are doing the same thing you have always done, but in a different way. Instead of getting rid of things, you just have them all around you and have put yourself in the closet instead. You are betrayed, because you keep betraying yourself.

You have chosen people in relationships that you would have to save, because they were a distraction from you stepping into your own power. Candace was important because you used her as the excuse to not be in your power. And you are still using her by hanging onto her creations. Who could you be if you let it all go, truly let her go, let the animosity go, and let yourself go? How powerful could you be? As long as those things surround you, regardless of how beautiful, you are in bondage to them. Deep down, all you really desire is to bond with others. Some part of you believes that these things maintain a bond, but in actuality, they keep you from bonding to your true Self."

Do not be mistaken; Love will push or prod you. It allows you to open when you are ready, but it holds the space. It offers you what you do not know. It bears no gifts, because Love knows you are the gift. It need not whisper to you, because it embraces you with the possibility of everything. Love asks nothing but allows for everything. Love supports you completely, bestowing an honor as its Beloved. Love does not want you to stay in hiding; it desires to share you with the world, to gift you to the world. Love is eternal and will wait for all eternity for you. Love will never leave you. It will continually empower you. The more committed you are to Love, the greater its ability to create a landscape that equals that commitment.

When we maintain barriers to keep people, life, or experience at a distance, or hide aspects of ourselves, we also block the degree of love and abundance available as support. When we wear masks to hide our feelings, we block our ability to intuitively feel into others and the intimacy of connection that creates joy and success. The world holds nothing from you. Love keeps nothing away. You keep it away from yourself.

Release the armor that you have encased yourself within. Your choice to take on a definition or demonstration of "doing love" as the concept of love was exactly that: a con. You created the armor as a means of protection, doing the best you could with what you had. It served its purpose, but now you can let that go. What rests underneath has not had the warmth, light, or tenderness that it needed. It can and will come. Love would not have it any other way. But Love would never rob you of the experience of fully feeling and immersing yourself in creation, allowing you to design and dance in what would feel loving. So, the next step is you get to redefine what being loved feels and looks like. As you give that to yourself, you experience the transmutation of the armor to amour—then Love will bring you all its reflections that match at the new frequency.

Do not hold back, especially from yourself. How much love can you stand? That is the question isn't it? We want it, but do not know how to handle it when we have it. To receive love and being loved is a process of unlearning. It is unlearning all of the defenses, projections, stories, and beliefs about what might happen, can happen, and will happen. That is a reflex to wearing armor for so long. Discipline yourself to receive Love, to be "in Love, of Love, and with Love" in every moment.

When you let yourself share all of who you are, you open to greater intimacy with all energy, in whatever forms it exists, and begin to experience a deeper awareness that Oneness is a possibility. At first, this is intellectual. Your willingness to discover it will begin to create experiences for embodying it. Your willingness connects other hearts to celebrating a more open way of sharing. The illusion will begin to morph into a new reality. Your new world requires radical honesty and uninhibited transparency.

The deeper you move into intimacy within the field of love—meaning openness and vulnerability—the more connected you will feel the field. Your internal landscape will strengthen, and you will wonder why you ever needed armor at all. The inner core will feel stronger than the armor ever did. This is your engagement to life. Next comes your reception as life unfolding and expanding.

As you continue to focus on your boundaries, recognize it has two faces. We can have boundaries on the outside to protect us and empower us. But we unconsciously created boundaries on the inside. Where are you wearing armor? What armor needs to be removed for you to fully allow life in? Your heart's desire...in? Your dream...in? It's time to remove the armor and transmute it to amour. When you fully let yourself in, you will be able to project yourself fully outward.

The one you have held armor in place against is yourself. It seemed to be with the outside world, but that is the illusion. There is no outside world. It all exists within. Just as a camera feeds the film through the inside of a projector, the light shines from behind it, but a lens projects it outward. The movie appears outward. For those who truly see, the cast and story has all been on the inside. There is and has never been anything out there, which is why it is so simple to change the picture. If you are guarded with armor, the picture will never change.

That place that lay between armor and amour is "experiencing." Open to the gentle rhythm of not-wanting-to-feel and not-feeling. This is how you will develop your intimacy. You have guarded yourself against the pain, but have you not felt some anyway? You have guarded yourself from heartbreak, but is that not what you have known? You hold a barrier between yourself and others to keep from feeling betrayed but as you do so, you betray the self that knows your truth. Let your self open. Be vulnerable. Embrace any and all experience. Those parts of you—the numb one, the guarded one, the broken-hearted one, the lonely one, the alone one—need the space to get to know their own steps. This is the dance, the flirtation with possibility and freedom. This is the dance of courtship between the separation of the self and the ONE Self. While they remain imprisoned within their own barriers, they cannot know the freedom that rests beyond.

Lay down your hardened shell, that armor you cast long ago. It has kept you sheltered and imprisoned, but is necessary no more. The war is over; you may be free. No more bondage or servitude. Time for the wounded to heal. You have nothing left to lose. The battlefield of the heart need be tended with care. Only Love can heal the bare-naked soul, whose truth is to openly share. From armor to amour.... May the romance begin.... Through life's churning.... Love, Courage, and Commitment allow another to way in.

YOU ARE INVITED TO

HAVE AND TO HOLD

TO HONOR AND CHERISH

REALIZING EVERYBODY BEING EXALTEDLY LOVED

AS THE PURITY AND PRESENCE OF

ESSENCE—VIBRATION—LIGHT—SOUND—HUE

BEING ONE NOW DIVINE

I AM THAT I AM

RSVP: REPRESENTING SOURCE'S VOLUMINOUS POWER

The Bridge From Replica to Rebel

How often do others celebrate you?

How many recognize your uniqueness?

Who encourages you to let your unique difference shine?

How often do you celebrate other people?

When they are going against the grain, do you support them or step back and wait, until you see others supporting them? Can you be truly happy for people when you see them happy, successful, and joy-filled? How do you experience and express that? Do you find yourself wanting to fit in?

How do you adapt or give yourself up to follow others in social, business, religious, or cultural ways, believing that is the only path because it is what the majority does? Do you want others to like you? Does it matter? Would you call yourself a replica or a rebel?

Not many want to see themselves as a replica, yet for whatever reason, do not desire to stand out as a rebel either. The majority would prefer staying in the safe confines of "normal." How does normal come about, and why? Have you ever thought about who "normal" really serves? Or does it create servitude? Does "the norm" help to bond? Or does it create forms of bondage? Does normal foster amour or support strengthening armor?

Most people just want to do what is needed to have a "little" happiness. It is easier not to fight the system. It is less taxing to be like everyone else. Somehow we begin to believe that fitting in so others like us is the key to success. The problem is, success has been defined in a very limited way. Most would define success as the material items possessed, the cars driven, home lived in, status attained, and labels worn. This endless ladder for more, better, higher, becomes the numbing wheel of addiction, leading to a robotic existence for many.

When fitting in becomes the norm, people begin talking the same, becoming clones of every new trend and living the same lives, even with the same dysfunctions. Each generation replicates this mindset, in addition to taking on the behaviors and surface emotion they have witnessed in others. People become wedged into mindless routines. Eventually they feel physically trapped between the attempt to keep up and the mounting debt. There are also those who appear successful but often times are more trapped, afraid to give up what they have even though it may no longer have meaning. In succumbing to the outside pressures and internal fears of loss, they are no longer present. These are the Stepford humans, living unconscious lives controlled by money, media, and other machines.

We fight strongly against the banking systems, drug companies, political parties and the Monsantos of the world. Don't you see they are merely the "in your face" representations of what you are creating in the world by becoming replicas of every system? It is all the same if you are just following trends and letting them have control of your uniqueness: the beauty industry, fashion industry, self-help industry, spiritual industry, sports, electronics—all of it! It is being marketed as a "we" concept. Is it really about you? Or, is it about them making you into them? I am not saying you should not support, enjoy, and engage. I am asking you not to lose yourself and follow along just because everyone else is. This is the way we subconsciously send the message that being unique is not as celebrated as being part of the clique. How we do one thing is how we do everything—just be aware.

I had a lot of time on my hands. I felt in every cell of my body that my life was going through a huge awakening process, and I desired to be present to every feeling and thought that rose up out of that. In stopping completely, I was given an opportunity to evaluate where some of my own frustrations had been. I asked out loud, "Show me what is burrowing in my core, ready to be revealed." I was not expecting what came next.

I received a call to be part of a joint venture. I had interviewed a woman about her work, and she had loved the interview. Through the years, whenever asked to promote certain events for her, I did. I had no fear of anything being taken from me, and some of the events I chose felt to be of good cause and intent. She was inviting me to be part of an event coming up, not as a speaker but as a host, because she liked my interviewing style.

Something about it did not feel right inside, but I said yes anyway. In the days following, I received affiliate links to promote the event, and she gave me the individuals she wanted interviewed. As I clicked on the link, I was surprised. She had listed her image and bio as the interviewer and, in a small line beneath, listed that I would be the host of that interview.

When I called to ask about this, she immediately dismissed it and said that was how this was structured so not to confuse attendees with too much information or too many names. I then asked if 11:11 could be listed as a free gift to all attendees, and there were no strings attached to it for them to buy anything else. This was my gift to humanity. Her reply was "Well, you would have to speak with the sponsor committee about the fees involved, but it could only go on the sponsor page. We just do not have the ability to promote anything that does not bring us revenue."

As I politely declined being part of her event, I went into my space of contemplation and was taken back to a couple of years prior. I had wanted my company to make a profit. I had a couple of products I promoted, but I give away most of what I create. Because the banks and others kept telling me I needed to do business in a certain way to have "success," I started engaging in their methods. Every step of the way, it did not feel good on the inside. I kept telling myself, "They are the ones that know. This is how it is done. All the leaders in the industry are said to follow these methods. I have to do the same. Okay...I will try this."

Very soon after, a dear friend contacted me and said, "You should do some of these tele-series. You can get your name out to a lot of people, you sell a product in bulk, and you will make a profit." The next thing I knew, she had booked me for a few events and was coaching me on creating the products to support it. I worked really *hard and spent weeks creating products. When I finished, she said to put a price on it. So I did. Then she said, "No, that is not enough; we need to include more. You need to have a lot to give away, and it needs to appear like you are giving thousands of dollars worth of value but then we are going to reduce it to $97."*

I could feel the upset inside of me, the "NO, NO, NO. This does not feel right." She very gently tried to tell me that this was how the industry worked, and if I wanted to be anybody, I had to follow along. Sick to my stomach, I agreed.

I did three series that autumn and literally was sick after each one. Work that I valued was being inflated and then drastically reduced, and it just felt icky. Where was the integrity, the trust, the truthfulness—especially in this "industry"? Mind you, this happens in many industries; I just happen to be in the inspirational field. I am not targeting them; this is just where my experience is. I am also not saying any of these people are bad or even had misaligned intentions. I do feel they were doing the best they could with what they had. They were operating from fear and lack, but I could not see that in that moment.

By the time I finished the third series and turned in the product for the purchasers, I was in the red. Between 50 to 70 percent going to the host of the series and 25 percent going to the broker and the cost of the physical product to be made, I spent $2,500 out of pocket. What was worse was how the experience felt. I knew this was not in line with who I wanted to be; it was just not resonating. I decided I would not be doing anymore of those. I would much rather create gifts to the world out of pocket and freely share them than feel what I felt here.

As I looked back, this also had to with beliefs on money and success. What I discovered was a huge AHA! My belief that I had to measure up in some way, the only real way being money, drove a fear within that I was not good enough because I was not doing it right. I realized I was in pure happiness when creating 11:11, which I give away. How had I created that all these years?

Somehow what I needed always showed up. I was not lacking for anything. When I looked at what I needed money for, I could not really determine an answer. When I do have money, I tend to give it away or help people with it in some way. So if I was just trying to make money to give it away in the end, what was the point? Then it hit me: we are all natural philanthropists. Our joy and happiness comes from helping others full-heartedly and being in service. That can be done in a multitude of ways and does not really require a ton of money to do so. I had become a spiritual replica of what had infiltrated the self-help industry from other industries. And although it may have initially been well-intentioned, it was grounded in fear and lack. How much do we really need? Why? What are we doing with all of it when we have it? And when we have that much, is it really filling us with what we wanted? Or, are we becoming slave to it and replicating slaves along the way?

Regardless of the industry, we have been programmed into the "me, me, me" concept, although our internal guidance keeps saying "NO! It is about the 'we, we, we'!" If it's "me, me, me," it is bathed in "fear, fear, fear." This belief that we must present ourselves behind the facades of false deals or manipulative packaging is actually a belief in lack and limitation. No wonder the law of attraction appears not to work for most. If the feeling beneath whatever you are doing is not resonating with who you are, it cannot bring about the success you are seeking, in any form. It is the small child trying to survive because he does not fully believe or trust in the world or himself. The small self is crying out and throwing a tantrum.

If it is "WE, WE, WE," it stands in love and the Greater Collective Self rises. This form of engagement supports those involved in a win-win, rather than compromising one or the other. The "WE, WE, WE" will organically move into the ALL, the emersion of the Divine Essence that expands the Creative Capacity that is Self-Organizing Unified Creation Expanding, also known as S-O-U-R-C-E.

When we move from "What's in it for me?" to "What part of me is in this?" not only do we discover our true motives, but world paradigms shift!

Am I judging and condemning people for what they are doing? Are money and the material "bad"? Am I saying these things are wrong? Do I want these industries to stop? No. I am asking you to look at and feel into what truly resonates with you, whether your ways truly align with your deepest self. When you see anything, participate, and utilize tactics, do they align with you? Do you follow suit and replicate ideas in your life and business because it is what everyone else does? Do you participate in practices that do not feel good but believe that is the only way? Are you so anchored in their business, that you are not present to your own, literally and figuratively? Is it time for a new program?

In succumbing to the programming that bombards us, we become endless consumer gluttons, never feeling fully satisfied because the outside world is filling up, instead of the inside world. We believe our fulfillment rests in another piece of jewelry, a new sofa, an art piece...a new car, the latest phone, another house...a new relationship, a cosmetic procedure, another workshop. It is all material—not truly necessary, but that which quickly becomes the drug. The more we take, the more is needed. The greater the consumption, the less individuated we are. And the world of commerce knows this and uses it. They are not in question; however, we are. What I am asking you is this:

- How conscious are you being? Or are you simply following suit, unconsciously?
- Are you a follower or experiencing yourself?
- Are you buying into someone else's voice or allowing your own to come through the experience of another's?
- Are you a replica?
- What about you makes you individual?
- What unique genius are you allowing and expressing?

The empty internal feeling and crumbling external world are only illustrating the weighted scale of one side. What balances the world is the uniqueness that is expressed. What solves the world's ills is the creation and voice each individual brings. What makes up ONENESS is ALLNESS. The ONE can only be fully experienced when we each bring forward that integral individuation of the ONE in a conscious, whole-hearted, expressive way. Consumption is not bringing us together; it is keeping us cloned. Clones cannot connect because they do not think or feel for themselves; they think and feel to be like everyone else, and that is the deepest form of betrayal. This ripples out in the world as forms of betrayal and experiences of being betrayed. Manipulation of our personas to fit in can only reflect as manipulation to and from one another. Massive consumption and waste are a mirror to how we are consumed and the waste of creative capacity that rests untapped in our world. And all the while we feel trapped, bound, bored, frustrated and in servitude.

The "more and more" we have creates a feeling of claustrophobia that we do not understand and this is projected onto the people closest to us in our lives. As the material becomes the Master, we become slaves to it. The unspoken conversation from the ego to the small self is *"When you have enough, you will be free."* Yet, our spirits know inherently, *"If I just free myself, I will have enough."* This is the angst. There is a knowing inside that keeps tugging, even while we continue to clamor outside for more. This knowing is patient and understands a moment will rise where the mountain of material gain and the ladder of social climbing will extend so high that it can only fall, bringing us back to the ground upon which we walk—back to our true selves.

Until that time, the greater Self will love us enough to let us have the truth that we are choosing. You have freedom, no matter how you try to imprison yourself. Your freedom is that you can make anything your truth. In the past, you have allowed both the disempowering story, as well as the empowered moments. As you proceed, discern carefully what you now choose to have as your truth.

Is your truth going to be the words of another, replicating those lauded as the epitome of success? Did you misinterpret what you were to replicate? It was not that you were to copy them or their lives. They need really be lauded for the example they set by standing in their voice and expression, their unique individual truth. Realize that a struggle likely existed as they built the confidence for outward expression. The day will come when an authority applauds you for your work or creation. Only then will you understand that you let yourself be fooled by society. Much as you believe otherwise, society is not trying to stifle you or stop you from being you. Society has created the perfect pressure cooker for you to eventually choose you.

What I do know is that all people are seeking experience. They want to connect and be a part of something meaningful. Every person desires to impact the world in some way. Every person wants to share their voice. Doing this in any way, large or small, is the true measure of success, and it has nothing to do with the material aspect of the world. Success can truly only be measured in the heart, and it is as individual as we each are.

Pioneers are not often recognized until they can show some results. Praise cannot be given until you are willing to appraise yourself and your life, making the necessary changes. People in your life will support you by giving you every reason to remain in the safe confines of replication, of lower conscious copy-catting.

It is essential to live your truth, especially when others do not understand. Your truth cannot have an effect if it goes unspoken, or if not acted upon. Naysayers simply do not have the capacity to see as far. Where would we be if people did not question systems? Where would we be if people such as Gandhi, Martin Luther King, Rosa Parks, Mother Teresa, Einstein, John Lennon, and Jesus did not speak and live their truth?

When you see someone being different, pioneering a new way, striking out on a new path, what do you do? Do you question it? Do you judge it? Are you jealous? Do you gossip? Do you speak about their failure or their success? Do you condemn them for doing what you have not had the will or courage to do? Or, do you make them your next false idol, because everyone else is doing so? This is how we keep everyone in line. Look around at the cliques and circles, the egos and "ego-nomics," the control and the controlled.

This has been the unfolding experience of the human condition and now it is self-organizing. These people that have kept you

walking single file, at attention rather than in your own full intention, have served. Everything serves.

Bless those that surround you. They are angels in disguise. They
are here specifically to pull you off course of your original destiny.
They have been a gift in the way they challenge you, have you doubt
yourself, trigger and hurt you. In doing so, they provided a more
lush landscape of experience. They are the compass that guides
you, both off course and back on. Those outside of you, in some
way, keep you seeking. Because of them, you have settled for less of
you. Also, if it weren't for these people, you would remain settling
for less of you. They may have kept you limited, but in doing so,
you are boomeranging back to yourself, your Greater Self. Because
of them, you take hold of your center, your truth, your voice, your
rights, and your knowing. In the end, all moving objects return to
center; all moving objects become still.

As you choose to walk your authentic path, people may point
fingers in judgment, engage in gossip, step back from you, abandon
your relationship, and pretend they do not know you. This is their
fear—of your power, of themselves, their own power, their world,
and the discovery of their false self. They may discover they are nobody, and as they look around, that they have become everybody.

**We are equally special and equally not so. Once we get beyond
that knowing, we can get to living, loving, and celebrating one
another for that.**

When we move from being a society that loves drama, pointing
fingers, and engaging in gossip, to one that has compassion, celebrates one another without fear of personal loss, and lives authentically, the ills of the world will no longer be present, because we will
stop being the disease. What we see outside is the world trying to
show us who we are being. Who are you being? The truth is you are

Divine. You are an individuation of the Divine Presence. Do not show up less than that! Others are that as well. They just have not awakened from their replicated existence.

Accept others where they are, with compassion. If they cannot see you, what you share and how you walk in the world, that is not your problem or a problem with your vision. Their own vision may have the glitch. They could be shortsighted in how to move, connect, grow, or expand. They might be farsighted, seeking an end result rather than engaging as experience. They may not have the courage to dive into the organic process of unfolding by saying yes to something unknown. They may not yet understand it. Nonetheless, do not cloud your vision because they cannot see. Do not stop speaking simply because they cannot hear. Do not stop walking because they cannot keep up. That is their experience as the journey, and it too will evolve, just like you.

How could you possibly know how others see you? They wear filters from wounds, upbringing, beliefs, and needs. When they see you, they cannot fully see you. They only see the projected aspect of themselves they have yet to know. Once they discover that, they will be able to see you as you are—not as they are.

Your purpose in life is to allow the unfolding of each present moment as the full experience that you are. When you hold back or doubt, or when you are half-hearted, the world will speak back in the same manner. Imagine how the world would speak to you if you were in full love, service, and commitment to your deepest heart desire in this present moment. Every piece and part of the world would self-organize to fulfill that prophecy. You are that. The question is, will you allow that?

You have permission to do whatever you want whenever you want. You willingly give that up.

What is the great mystery of the world? YOU are! The possibility you hold, the expanse of creation you possess, the love you can exude, all the mystery of you—you are the untapped magic in the world. You hold an individual piece of genius from the Great Mind. Instead of questioning everything around you, take the questions inside; involve and evolve in the mystery! That will become your Mastery.

The genius you hold will never look or sound like anyone else's. It is why it is your unique genius. The planet needs that. Do not place pressure upon yourself as if life is something to do. It is what you are to BE. From your Being, the Doing will rise.

Identify your truth. No one else will know that but you. No one may understand it. The real way to illustrate that authentic expression is by being the example of that truth, completely uninhibited. Then, you will show up in the way that serves your soul. You will stand apart from the army of clones society has unconsciously created.

This holographic world is filled with people, representations of the many pieces of you asking to be released. They need for you to live as an individuation of Divine Truth: as the inspiration, an intimidation, the one to be jealous of, the teacher, the friend, and the collaborator. Regardless of the way they respond, how they label your actions or see you, their opinions, reactions, and responses are not your focus or business. These are merely perceptions through their filters and a message of what needs to be released from you, so they may be free. Everyone has human filters. The only real spiritual purpose is to live and be the conscious example and experience. That is the walk of the Master—through sunflower fields, murky marshes, and rocky mountains, and amongst the stars—all sacred spaces.

How do you know when you have found your true Self? You awaken to having been lost. What is defining the moment between lost and Divine Knowing? You give to the Self the greatest truth of all. You are a walking, breathing, creating aspect of the Divine. The Man and the Mana!

You never have to scream or shout your truth. It does not even need to be spoken, not even a whisper. Your truth will be self-evident; it will be lived and embodied. That will be its loud-speaker, its megaphone. When something speaks that evidently, it cannot be ignored, denied, or go unheard. Your living truth will ripple out in ways you cannot see, imagine, or fathom. It's rippling should not even be of concern. Just BE your truth—for no one else but you! There is only ONE here...and it is YOU! When you choose to fully embody that, boldly expressing your heart and soul, your dreams and desires, you are choosing the path of the Rebel.

The Rebel lives in a constant unfolding potentiality, without attachment to anything, but in wonder and discovery of everything. The Rebel is not fighting against anybody or anything. In fact, they are not even interested in the outcome. It is about the experience of creation. There are no goals. The result does not matter. The only thing that matters is the experience of full love, courage, and commitment to something greater than the small self. Because of that, an automatic and Divine flow leads to what is the best outcome.

They are awake and aware, but glide as a magnetizing movement, catalyzing others to stand in their true power as well. Rebels free themselves and their experience through the conscious growth of their own destiny. In walking such an authentic path of devotion, the inherent gifts locked within the DNA and RNA structures of the cells are awakened through a series of organically opening physiological and energetic processes. The Rebel's ability to be true to their soul is their self-created awakening and the activation to these bodily gateways.

The world's powerful turning point is predicated on individuals willing to be Rebels, which awakens Mastery of multidimensional experience. Rebels do not have a need or desire to control. They rest securely in trust and intimacy with all that exists. The Rebel is loyal and devoted, building movements and communities. Beautiful and holy, The Rebel Road is a sacred path that will transform today's human into the unfolding of the awake and aware Hue-man. There is a very ancient, deep part of every human being that is ready to take The Rebel Road.

We are no longer wounded. That is story.

We are Masters. We have always been.

It is time to awaken to the Light and Truth of that.

It is the moment to awaken to the play of Hue-mans.

This is the moment. This is Moment-US!

The Rebel travels a road that few have known. It appears, to the outside, one of risk, perhaps even insanity, but it is all in sanity. Many may judge because they have become enamored by their illusions, so caught in their need to belong. The allure of *maya*, the norm of physicality, is a strong manipulator that they cannot see beyond. How can they know that the degree of attachment to "what they have" and "who they are" keeps them feeling alone and afraid? Every attachment and possession builds on and creates fear, loss, and death. This is what it means to be "possessed."

Humanity's greatest fear is death or disappearance...
How strongly are you clinging to everything you know and have?
To what degree are you in bondage?
To what degree are you possessed?

Rebels do not have attachments. Who they are is not dependent on what they have, degrees attained, or number of digits in a bank account. It is not reflective of a political or religious affiliation. Their lives are solely based on experience and expansion and the communal bonding with more of themselves. The side effect created by the Rebel is loyalty, union, and communion. Their heart and passion for the effervescent bond of life is their magnet. This wealth of passion and heart attracts everything that continually radiates their "feel"-d of Love.

The Rebel does not travel alone. The Divine Beloved is actively playing with and providing for the Rebel every step of the way, continually teasing her to unlock the mystery, and asking her to step fully into Mastery as she meanders through. The Rebel knows that life is meant to be a co-creative adventure and is willing to live that experience out fully. Rebels listen and look for the conversations from the Universe, knowing they are ever guiding and present.

There is no fear of loss and death, because the Rebel knows that settling and feeling trapped is death and loss of the self. He transmutes fear into a new experience, one that is defined in a new way: F E A R = Feeling Excited About Reality! No fear, in the traditionally defined way, exists. The excitement present is not bouncing off the walls; it is one that is energized but grounded in trust.

The Rebel has left behind the life of bondage, servitude, guardedness, and replication. There are no attachments to things, opinions, identities, beliefs, or ways of being. It is full-fledged exploration and continual bonding of what IS within and all the expressions of that Divinity that IS outside, even with those that "know not what they do." It is the beginning stages of anchoring into and accepting the invitation to know "I AM that I AM. WE are that WE are."

This is not pressure to do or be anything...

This is an invitation, to be accepted or denied.

You are the ONE invited...

But, you must be the ONE that extends the invitation.

And, YOU would be the ONE that accepts it.

~

YOU ARE INVITED TO

RELEASE, RECREATE, AND REMEMBER

YOUR ORIGINAL BEING

YOUR CHILDLIKE WONDER

YOUR INNOCENCE AND IMAGINATION TO

DREAM—PLAY—LAUGH—SING—DANCE—COLOR

WITHIN THE PLAYGROUND OF LIGHT AND SOUND

BRIGHTLY EXPANDING AND ILLUMINATING PASSIONATE EXPRESSION IN

UNIQUE DIVINE GENIUS

RSVP: REACTIVATING SELF-ORGANIZING VICTORIOUS POSSIBILITIES

~

The Awakening of the Bridge: An Activation

The bridge anchors deep and strong, rising and regal, carrying many across a wide expanse of unknown, always beginning and ending at a place which meets others where they are.

It is my willing and open-hearted intention to...

Allow my being to expand and evolve beyond any and all limiting perceptions, influences, and filters.

Walk an aligned path of authentic living and conscious co-creative intention.

Accept and embrace that I have created my experience and can create a new one at any moment.

Kindly and gently let go of the identities, personalities, and fears that no longer serve me in a loving manner.

Embrace my voice, power, and presence as valuable and necessary in the world.

Navigate the earth plane, expressing the confidence and creativity of my unique genius, in service with Love, for the purposes of bonding to one and all.

Make mature, clear, grounded choices that serve my highest good.

Encourage myself to play with childlike wonder every step of the way.

Bridge the gaps of your life, not by creating something new, but in extending who you already are. Strong bridges anchor deep but rise high above common ground. They meet us where we are but support us in crossing over. Be the bridge. Anchor deeply in your truth. Light the way, meeting people where they are with love, compassion, and kindness after you have done this for yourself.

Play in the Light of Gratitude

I

want to

play with you.

Got you! You're it!

Let's pretend... I'll go first!

I can't wait to open it! Look what I got!

We have forgotten the essence of our nature,

the ability to be joyful, playful and spontaneous.

Childlike innocence and wonderment are essential

to connecting to the full expanse of our Divine Essence.

Too many of us have forgotten how to play.

We have lost that connection and the meaning

of being children of the Universe.

We have also forgotten

the integrative experience of many words

such as gratitude, love, and compassion.

We have become grounded in work...

working hard,

working on others,

working on ourselves.

WE have forgotten to play.

We have forgotten *how* to play.

It is time to remember.

Will you play

with

me

?

Gratitude is the best part of the game of life. It is where we meet and connect. It is the clasping of hands, the high five, and the celebration after the big win. Gratitude is GREAT FULLNESS. It is the Divine Spark recognizing itself in another being, experience, or way. When in gratitude, individuated Light expands and extends beyond the body, meeting another body of Light in an illuminated embrace. In that moment, the whole Universe Lights up, the heavens sing, and all hearts rejoice at the unity that creates a GREAT FULL moment of ONENESS.

Tag! You're it!

Do you remember playing tag? Everyone would scurry around the playground trying not to get caught but wanting to. To the runners, the one that was "it" had the most fun. I remember secretly wanting to be caught just so I could be "it." I think the others did too. We wanted to be "it," until we were. Then of course, we wanted to be the ones running, especially if we could not catch anyone.

Remember having chased everyone for so long, hoping you would just scrape the edge of a shirt or a finger would graze an arm so you could yell, "YOU'RE IT!" How invigorating...and again how great and full we were. Remember what it was like to tag someone? Awesome! It was like winning the game. Remember the feeling of finally being tagged! The excitement, the YAY! It was like winning the game. We were never down about being tagged. It was exciting! We were actually happy and filled up—great full—at being tagged. Children see the win-win in situations. They want to be all parts and engage fully when they are. They just want to experience the game. Remember the gratitude regardless of the position...the gratitude was there every step of the way because the present moment was there every step of the way.

What if life were approached like a game of tag. In a moment's notice, we simply are "it"—the lover or the broken hearted, the winner or the loser, the one in power or the victim—it's all a game and we get to take turns being "it." Whatever situation is happening in your life, you are getting to play the game. Be in the present moment with full gratitude. Each time you are tagged or tag, have gratitude for the new experience about to be engaged in. "TAG! YOU'RE IT!"

Look back over your life and celebrate your scorecard! Were you were able to experience both sides of an experience? That is the beauty of the game of life: health and sickness, wealth and debt, gain and loss, success and failure, love and heartbreak, birth and death.

Patty-Cake, Patty-Cake: Let's Pretend! I'll Go First!

Remember playing "Patty-cake patty-cake, baker's man. Bake me a cake as fast as you can. Pat it, prick it, and mark it with a 'B.' Put it in the oven for baby and me!"

The hands come together two by two creating unity. A clap of gratitude sounds as they celebrate and extend Namaste. They continue play, as their palms meet in a mutual exaltation of "The Divine in me acknowledges the Divine in you." They meet in one another fully present, continually taking the experience to a faster pace, a higher vibration. The "cake we bake" is the sweetness of life. Of course, it would be branded with a "B" to glorify the Beloved.

Patty-cake is a beautiful metaphor for remembering why we have come: to engage deeply with one another, in the play of the small self and the Greater Self—the mother and the child, the soul and its mate, the Lover and Beloved.

What is it that you are creating with this playmate of life; this one who sees and knows you so intimately? The Great ONE you engage with in all experiences from being wounded to finding power as it expresses in many forms within and without. There is no judgment, only the willingness to experience everything to the fullest, knowing the Divine as all expression. In this game of life, who plays and has played together?

Look back over your life and celebrate your score card! Were you were able to experience both expressions of the Divine? That is the beauty of the game of life: judge(d) and forgiver(n), controller and compromiser, co-dependent and independent, addicted and free, selfish and selfless, arrogant and humble, weak and strong.

Cracker Jacks: I Can't Wait to Open It! Look What I Got!

The joy of surprise! Is it the sound of something shaking inside? It is the mystery of the unknown? Perhaps it is the gift amongst all the caramel corn. Would Cracker Jacks taste as sweet if there were not a prize inside? I think not. It does not matter whether it is a Cracker Jacks box, a gumball machine, or games at a county fair, anytime there is a prize—an unknown one at that—excitement bubbles!

As a kid, those little trinkets that hardly cost more than a few cents, hidden inside a box of sugary corn are like winning the lottery. And even after we find it, what is so great is that we still get to nibble on delicious sweetness.

Why can't we look at life like that? After all, could the world not be a box of Cracker Jacks? Perhaps we are here to move through the sticky and the sweet, the nutty and the hard, to find the gift. Or better yet, maybe we are the actual gift amongst all of life. From a child's eyes, if we took it a step further, maybe the whole box of life is just full of the prizes and surprises! And the one piece of caramel corn, well that is just holding the space for more to come! In this game of life, are you savoring the prizes and surprises?

I am the one who plays.

I am a child of the Universe, a Divine ONE.

My laughter lights up the world.

My song is the sound of creation.

*I am the Divine Devilish One who creates mischief
with a sly smile.*

*I am the Divine Angelic One that embraces
with a compassionate eye.*

I am the Divine Godly One creating in Love in every moment.

*I am the Divine Scale of Balance that also
disciplines my experience.*

I am the Light that is to color this world.

I am the harmony that rises once all sound is heard.

I am the space of the unknown...waiting to become known.

The truth is out!

THE INVOCATION

It is all you. Everything. All of it. As infants, we come in knowing and seeing the truth of who we are. We engage with delight and wonder at the magic all around us, because we feel in play with it. There is an intimate comfort-ability with both, the seen and unseen. There are coos and giggles as the eyes dance with things that adults no longer see or recognize. There is as much presence and Godliness in sleep as there is in moments awake. We are open, knowing no boundaries between our bodies and the world. We see everything in play with us, as a part of US. It is shimmering Light, sound, and color, and we desire to be with it all.

In becoming toddlers, there is an innate curiosity that engages us. We are in the moment, experiencing everything with exalted curiosity. Our emotions are things we also play with, laughing one moment and a tantrum the next, as we skip off playfully in the next moment. We are not attached to the emotions or to the things that caused them. We are experience, completely present in the moment, engaged with the body and the world as one. Knowing there is no separation in the world around us, there is no fear. We continue being open, and in doing so, we continue to feel all that is Light, in addition to feeling all that is distortion of the Light. In knowing that it is all One, we soak up all that is felt, making it more of our truth.

Distortions of the Light condition us into learning someone else's truth, feeling someone else's energy, and taking on others' feelings. The distortion is heavy and takes up space within us. It begins to weigh upon the parts of us where it embeds itself. We begin to identify ourselves as certain experiences rather than all experience experiencing itself. We are taught how to think, what to believe, and when to feel. We are told to grow up, behave, sit still, and pay attention. An understanding forms, through what is spoken and unspoken, to follow the rules of the one who is dominant. We become controlled and no longer free. Life turns into a schedule to follow instead of an adventure to awaken to. Each day is something to navigate, rather than travel within. Each moment becomes more of a question, as we fall farther and farther into amnesia.

The Light does not disappear, nor does it dim; we simply step into the shadow of it. As a lantern in the fog, it beckons. We see no difference in the playing field because we learn mechanisms to survive. Our brilliance appears as creative adaptability. Even amidst chaos, we continue to play. We find the moments that we can fill with song and laughter. Innately we are all children of the Universe, playing in the fog that surrounds us. The density of the mist is enamoring, as we dance inside distortions of the Light. Within that darkness, the Light still shines. It appears overhead as something above us, outside of and away from us. It is the first significant disconnect as we separate from the Self.

In the midst of dress-up, we forget we are playing, slowly losing a sense of the detached innocence and aliveness that was innate. The lie becomes our truth. "Being" turns into doing. The illusion feels like reality, and this is how we begin to know ourselves. Dress-up becomes identity; we forget we are playing and make our new surroundings a reality. However, regardless of the ways we create separation, this can never be. The infinite field will bring waves of Love until all those adrift, lost at seeing, come face to face with the sands of time. Life's churning waters will send us to a distant shore, not knowing who or where or when or why we are. The limited knowing that exists barely keeps us afloat. The moment arises when we allow ourselves to fully surrender to the "current" that exists. The pull is strong and takes us deep, into the dark waters. We have been fighting to survive in an ocean, never understanding we are the ocean and everything in it.

Although the dark seems bleak and never-ending, it is actually the place where the waves toss and turn us. The depths that we let ourselves sink to allow us to drown in the motion and finally die. That is when we float again to the top, seeing the Light, landing on the shore. Although it appears to have been a death, it is not. It is a chance to begin again. This can only come when we decide, once again, to reclaim our lost innocence, letting go of the imaginary kingdom that has been created for the real one that lay before us.

When in surrender to the mystery, the process of unlearning may begin. There will come a point for each person to choose to release knowledge and belief. Learning, knowing, and unlearning are the steps into the unknown, for discovering the unknown self. In the UNKNOWN, we discover the innate beauty that is the greatness we each began with.

Allowing ourselves to kneel, crawl, and once again be willing to roll upon the earth, light-hearted, full of wonder and discovery, we have the ability to lose sense of the seriousness, the callousness that has been building over time. This callus expands and hardens from the abrasions of life's experience. It is the hard edge of survival built up by what we chose to believe. It is the deadness of living with and carrying the emotional baggage of others. It appeared as protection until we could awaken to knowing there was nothing we need be protected from.

From belly to four-legged and then on two, we experience the human condition. That often leads us back to four legs, finding our knees to the ground, as we encounter the dark night of the soul. Then, we hobble along on three, two legs and the staff of unforgiveness that remains, until we are once again on our backs staring at the vastness that we are as the Universe. The chance for recognition comes as a wake-up call while in the human experience. Life grates away at the callousness held.

In the steps of self-love, tending to the tender spots that rest beneath the hardened places of life, we meet our vulnerability. At first, it is a surprise even to the one experiencing. They have not even known themselves; they have not really known the softness that rests beneath. They do not have any idea how to celebrate and honor that side, because it is not what the world celebrates. The world has forgotten how to be real. It has been stripped of its original mission and voice, and turned into the hardened expression of many carrying the lie that we have to fight for survival. What we need to outlive is our belief that life is as cold and hard as the callus.

There is, in fact, nothing to survive. We are either dead or alive, but we are "always." We simply exist, in one form or another. We exist and that cannot change. We are either in physical form as humanity, in spirit form as celestial beings, in energy form as space and time; we are in whatever form we choose for growth, experience, and evolution. We are "always," in all ways. We bought into many lies.

This idea will either expand you, or you will fight believing in it. How does knowing this truth serve you? How does fighting this truth serve you? It all serves, because it never has been about survival. Everything supports experience and your willingness to embrace increasing levels of it. You have as much right to suffer as you do to be in joy. Whichever you most desire will be granted because it is all YOU, conspiring to create what you most desire to experience.

Regardless of what you choose to have, reconciliation occurs while in the transition phase between human and universal God-being. Full remembrance and unconditional Love occur when united in the full God-being. Full power and celebration return when you do. You are always at play. On earth, you are in active physical play.

A child dives fully into life because they are alive. They ask for everything because they know they can have anything. They believe and trust the world was created for them. They embody Light, sound, and color. They only know love and they embrace everything with it. They only know courage. They live their emotions from the heart, not the mind. Their only commitment is to the present moment experience.

These are the true teachers of creation. This teacher exists inside each and every one. We have not lost this Divine Child; it has stepped back. It need only be invoked. It is not that it has forgotten you; you have forgotten YOU, by believing you had to grow up. No one forced you to do that; you chose to. Now choose again. No one ever need grow up; they only need to show up, ready to play!

The Language of the Hue-Man

Language is always a clear sign as to where we come from and where we are going. Regardless of how a person is "dressed up," his language will betray his true appearance. He will unconsciously speak from his filters. If he is someone who has rehearsed his speech, it will be evident in his life. His true beliefs and motives will be reflected in his living. If he is coming from a truly authentic place, it will touch your heart. You may not know why you trust, but you will. There will be resonance. Life is beautiful in how it supplies checks along the way for those willing to discern.

There are distinct differences between the old paradigm and the new. Language is one of the most critical. Words and phrases will either stem from the mind or the heart. Old paradigm thinkers have two legs lodged in the human condition, belief in limitation, lack, and fear. The body feels in tension, while the head shakes, trying to figure out where the problems came from. The questions are:

- How does this get fixed?
- Who can we get to fix it?
- Who caused this?
- Who is to blame?
- What can we market as a solution?
- What agency needs to be created to "think" about this?
- Who do we "need" to serve here?
- We have to fight this!
- We have to stop this!

While the intellect has served to a certain degree, it is limited in its ability. Intellect roams about in the head, so language will always be steeped in the mind's filters. Within all of this is an undercurrent of fear, a lack of possibility, and very little trust. The intellect is quietly insecure, and although it knows a great deal, it has no knowledge that is integrative for the body. Information is collected and filed in the mind—in no way experienced—so it cannot be breathed and integrated fully.

Past language has been guided by the shadow. Internal filters based on fight or flight determines the language learned and used. In not wanting to face personal responsibility, the mind processes and equates what is outside by being caused from the outside. That only creates logical conclusions, leaving no room for anything beyond logic.

The intellect strengthens by using the voice of reason. The mind wants to define things. It needs to identify what is happening, name it, label it, and categorize it. This is the red tape of the mind and it often translates into the red tape of society. There is no room for flexibility, or respect for the unknown. The mind wants to control. Everything must be known or figured out. Otherwise it does what the mind knows to do; it files it away out of sight, until it pops up again as an even larger issue.

"What is A? What is B? Why do we want to get from one to the other? How do we get from point A to point B in the fastest way?"

The mind will want to use science and math. Everything must be explainable and measurable. The mind sets a timetable and a schedule. The mind has a plan and a path that is predetermined. In the head, everything is black or white, manipulated into shades of gray.

Old-paradigm "mind thinkers" will speak from an unconscious space of personal gain, money-making, status building, and recognition. The intellect will generalize and try to determine one path from many, constantly narrowing the field. The intellect is trained to rule things out to find the answers. It views language as a means of identification, placing little value on frequency of words or the weight of feeling.

The new paradigm is lived by those holding earth in the palms, close to the heart, knowing they are the solutions. These beings innately understand that solutions do not come by sitting across a table from one another, separated; they sit side by side, united. Thinking still occurs, but it is a space entered into farther along the way, after heart intelligence and core genius has felt into the focus at hand.

The New Dawn recognizes language as a key component for growth and connection. Heart intelligence takes precedence, guiding all decision-making. When it comes time for integration and action, the gut becomes fully engaged, unleashing core genius and power. "Thinking" for the new human is a process of feeling, listening, connection, body awakened intelligence, connection, listening, feeling, visioning, inspiration, action...and the cycle continues.

There is no rush. It is about the experience. The new human desires to be experience experiencing itself as the vast body of knowledge that comes forth, integrates, is inspired, creates, and inspires. That which is in the core and the heart is the central funnel of the "Torus" body system, allowing experience in, as, and through tapping into the inner, the outer, above, and below. The new human seeks to fully engage, multi-dimensionally.

Language is grounded in authenticity and freedom. It is centered and service-based, requiring less details and allowing more space. It is guided by a sense of empowerment. Because these individuals are courageous to face the Light and dark of themselves, the heart is strengthened by compassion, communication, and understanding. The New Human recognizes the outside world as a reflection of herself, not a problem to be fixed but an experience to be engaged with. The questions are spoken from a different place, utilizing a different energy. Notice how the language changes:

- What can be created here?
- How can I be the solution?
- Where is that in me?
- What new pathways have the possibility of birthing here?
- How may we connect as the answers?
- This is an opportunity for connection, birth, and creation.
- How does this serve?
- This is not a problem; it is an opportunity.
- How many ways may I engage with this, in mind, body, spirit, energetically, in unity and community?

Heart intelligence seeks integration of experiences within the body. The heart feels into things, witnessing what happens from an open space. It has no desire to control or manipulate. There is room for flexibility and respect for the unknown. For the heart, organic unfolding and the innate ability for nature to self-organize are exhilarating. The conversation sounds different: *"Hello, A? Hello, B? How can we engage with A and B? How do A and B serve? What is the experience that each piece and part is seeking to create? Can we come together in an experience that organically unfolds what has been unknown?"*

The heart will engage community through compassion. It seeks to serve the collective solutions. It is not interested in fame, fortune, or a spotlight. There does not need to be a plan or a path. It only asks for an experience of connection. The heart and soul wish to create with others, as a part of something meaningful and joyful with those who desire the same.

Within all of this is an undercurrent of love, a knowing of the nature of the Universe, and trust. The new-paradigm thinkers speak from a space of exchange, collaboration, equality, and service. The heart celebrates individuation, community building, and the creation of many paths from one. The heart embraces all things to inspire solutions, allowing time to support a natural unfolding. It views language as a means of connection and frequency, two vital elements in creating new realities.

There is a distinct difference between who we are and who we are becoming. As human beings transform back into full remembrance of being Light, they use a language befitting one who remembers. There will be those that dream and keep on dreaming. There are those who cannot dream because they have forgotten how. And then, there is the new human who realizes they are the dream to be embodied and expressed.

They open-heartedly align with creative sparks like themselves to create a new reality. They move beyond the fear and desperation of saying, "I want this for me. I want recognition. Follow my way," and into a space of "I know who I am and want to share that with the world in service. How can I connect with you so that we celebrate one another's expression? Let's meet in a play of creation, collaboration, and celebration! What can I do for you? How may I do this for us, for all? Let's create a win-win-win."

These people come from a place of knowing something new. They know inherently that something better is possible and are willing to connect with like minds to discover it. Their focus is not money, leadership, status, the spotlight, or any personal gain. They are soulfully driven by the ability to experience. Their motive is to BE the experience, have experiences, and know experience as the collective in community.

Those in the new paradigm do not judge others as good or bad. They honor all, knowing they will align with like-minded people. They are clear that we are not here to fix or save anything. They hold a resonance and space of action that is the change necessary to catalyze others. In compassion, they recognize some are where they are and that is okay. All others are just different frequencies, holding their own foundations and distinct motives. Every one remains where they are, until they are not.

Like the small child, we must learn this new language by feeling into and creating it along the way. Words are energies, just like actions and emotions. In being more cognizant of the words we use and how we use them, a new language will form. It will reflect clearly whether a person speaks from old-paradigm energy or that of a whole new world. Feel every word you speak and witness where in the body it comes from. Those that you fully feel in your heart and gut are likely to help develop this language and, in turn, the authentic action to amplify the vibrations of those very words into creation.

The child is always radically honest, something many have forgotten. They speak their truths, their in-the-moment thoughts and feelings with authenticity. They are not concerned with how anyone else is going to react, because they are grounded in their right to experience. They also let it go once it has been expressed. It is not carried or attached to. This is a learned behavior. They operate from feeling, not thinking. They move from the heart instead of the mind. They never question who to play with; they just play with whomever shows up in their sandbox.

The Culture of the Hue-Man

The new human moves from a different baseline than we have in the past. The focus is not on what happened to us, who we were, or who we are becoming. It is based on a present-moment awareness of who we are right now. We are not trying to be anything other than experience and presence. It has nothing to do with accomplishing goals or even setting them. There is no desire to place standards of measurement or achievement. Instead, life is an opportunity to create a way of being that honors and celebrates the vast landscape of various points *as* the journey.

The average human of the past has been dictated by one of three spectrums:

- Life was directed by who we were based on how we measured out: the degree attained, the size of the bank account, the material assets acquired, the number of Twitter followers, measurable stats, job status, and so on.

- Life was based on what needed to heal, the wounded self, the brokenness, seeing life through a mind that could not see beyond the past. Experiences, up until that point, were viewed as random occurrences, a mystery, in question and needing of answers.

- Life was something requiring a purpose relegated to teacher, healer, leader, soldier, worker, philanthropist, or evangelist here to help, enlighten, save, or fix.

All of these require leaders and followers, those seemingly empowered and disempowered. The best metaphor appears to be the onion. This is the encased, smelly onion that continually brings tears. It is filled with layer after layer of story and pain. Between the layers are thin veils that cannot be grasped or become the sticky substance we become entangled in. The farther we go in, the darker it gets and the greater the sting.

We are focused on the problems and walking blindly in the dark, so there is no way to see that we are the solution. Even though the mirrors that appear are showing us who we are, they appear cloudy and murky, so we turn from them rather than realizing they are the reflection of who we have been. They are a reflection that sheds Light, that turns us toward the Light, that helps us to Lighten up. But, we cannot because we take it all too seriously. We take everything to be too serious in nature.

There is a distinct but important fine line between the proverbial onion and the lotus flower. Those that see life as the onion travel a dark and multi-veiled path, which keeps going deeper and deeper. It is easy to get trapped in all the layers and stuck in the dark. This is the land of bondage, servitude, replication—where the armor forms. This has been the preferred metaphor for most people in their healing process, a limiting, disempowering one, unbeknownst to them. But they are this, because it is what has been taught. Wisdom is forsaken for knowledge, because the intent is to get rid of, heal, or fix the pain. The onion clearly is heavy, but the lotus offers the Light.

The seed that forms as the lotus flower continually rises. It does not seek the Light because it knows it is Light on some level. It is engaged with experiencing itself unfurling, growing, stretching, bursting through, and blossoming. Within the mud, it begins to understand these experiences are part of itself. It requires the mud, the cool moments, the darkness to mature and rest in. As it rises, it feels the tears, but there are moments of elation. As it begins to know itself, it can honor both. If focused on possibility instead of the problem, we can embrace moving in the dark as we become the solution. Instead of choosing to be blinded in the dark, we are open to being blinded by the Light. In bursting forth, we embrace the other lotus flowers where they are because, as mirrors, they speak to us. They help us gauge our experience. They help us know we are not alone. We can celebrate their blossoming while experiencing our own.

If you see yourself and your life as the lotus, then the mission is more about experiencing rather than healing. You are able to recognize the mud, muck, and mire as a beautiful beginning for growing, strengthening, rising, and blossoming as you continually move toward the Light. An opportunity to push through and blossom, fully basking in the sun, is empowering. Perhaps Light shows up when we show up, regardless of where we are or what experience we are engaged in. LOTUS: Living Oneness Today Unveiling Source.

When the metaphor for life is the lotus flower, it is all inclusive. The flower recognizes it could not have blossomed without its surroundings, the cold, the dark, the sun, or the air to breathe. There are no questions because we know we are the answer.

- Where will you let your mind go today?
- Will it see life as an onion or see itself as the lotus?
- Will you be limited by the past or empowered by the experiences you overcame?
- Will you choose to play within your surroundings or are you constantly working through things?
- Do you view from the perspective of creating something new? Or healing something old?
- Do you go crazy, trying to find an answer? Or, do you understand that you are the answer?

- Can you open your mind, heart, soul, hands, and being to ALL-possibility and see what flows in?

- Are you ready to play in the land of ALL-possibility?

The child's culture is to feel. The heart must feel; that is its purpose. It was given as the very mechanism of integration and expression. You came for this experience. Do not deny it this beauty of feeling every emotion to the fullest. This expanse of experience for the heart is rich and beautiful. Do not judge the emotions you have. They are the buffet of soul experience, all delicious and with their own flavor. Taste every bit of life to the fullest.

When the morning dawns, you also dawn anew. Will you have a new day, new vision, new Light? A child does not bring one minute into the next, much less a day, week, or year. Will you bring yesterday in and cling to the old? When night comes, do you put to bed the day's experiences, retire anything that requires completion, and close your eyes to all that is illusion? After all, that was the day's dream. You easily forget and move past nightly dreams. Why do you cling to the ones you experience during the day? They are simply that: day dreams, illusions of play. Or, do you hold them and carry them into your night dreams, distorting your jaunt into the heavens? The subconscious sometimes works overtime in an attempt to support us through all the story and emotion held from experiences. Night dreams end up being for the purposes of working through issues instead of the opportunity to plug in to the Allness that exists. Let each day dream and each night dream have a beginning and an end. You are here to live each moment anew, allowing every experience to have a dawn and a closing.

The New Dawn asks humanity to embody a new culture. The manner in which we do things has to move beyond our human nature, but be reflective of Divine Nature.

Currently, we are problem-focused, using quick fixes and seeing everything as the onion needing healing. Answers feed the problems by dumping money towards them, which tends to enlarge the problems. Instead of pulling out our wallets, let us place forward our hands and engage. Let's extend our hearts. Let's discover new resources and forms of exchange.

Why is the world in debt? Money has become more about power than exchange. Minds are more focused on excess rather than access. When we move back into the energy of exchange, abundance of all types will begin surfacing. The metaphysical equivalent to money is relationship. We are in debt because we are not engaging in relationship. We are engaging in problems and paper, instead of people and possibility.

The new paradigm asks us to move from a world of disconnection to connection; from a replicated, numb society to creative Rebels coming together. Instead of living in our heads, we are to live out our hearts, every experience fully engaged, fully feeling. It is time to allow the heart its full purpose. Emotion is necessary because we are energy in motion. We are to swim *through* emotions—not over them, not around them, and not past them. This new culture is asking you to be intimate with emotion, embracing the illusions you have created, by feeling, breathing, allowing, and letting go.

Due to generations of suppressed pain and disempowering behaviors, the new human is asked to transition the world to its full embrace of Divine Knowing by feeling through things that rise up. We are to feel and release. At the very foundation of all emotion will be sadness, as it holds the greatest density. There is a role each individual plays in the massive cleanup of our world; it begins with the massive cleanup of the inner worlds.

Sadness is the place deep in the heart where separation first occurred. The place of betrayal encompasses the dreams you did not allow or that did not end in the fairy tale you had hoped for. But this is also the cushion of the Divine, the deep palm that holds you. When you reach the bottom of yourself, you discover the Divine. If you let yourself slip deep into this sadness, you will find the Divine holding you tenderly, embracing you with the deepest love and cherishing you in the way you have always desired. If you want that feeling to truly unfold, give it to yourself. That is the manner in which the Divine may truly express. When you allow any experience, it rises up and out and will not remain as is meant to be. In living this way, we cannot be affected by illness or aging. We would forever remain children. It is our attachment and emotional density that creates age and dis-ease.

Every single thing in life is an expression of Love and Light, even the hard, painful, and challenging. There is only Love and Light or varying distortions of them, here to reveal themselves. As you become aware of the distortions, bringing higher levels of your Light and Love to then, the awareness of them become part of your true self.

By loving the moments that you consider unloving, you meet a child that was never allowed to express as a child would. In having space to be witnessed, the previously unacknowledged child will step behind you instead of acting out in front of you. You will see his powerful self is still there and never left. The powerful self stepped aside in love for the rest of you, to bring the rest of you to the Light of yourself. Once the child is given the moment to feel, he will skip off to play once again.

Because we are coming from a paradigm of holding on to the past and having attachments, there will be periods of acknowledging disempowered aspects. Experiences of present-moment living will be more sensory. When attachments from the past arise, you can be with them and finally let them go. In time, you will only live in present-moment awareness and will have stepped into the culture of the new human.

If you were to live only in the present moment, never going to the past, not worrying or projecting into the future, the only thing you would experience is...YOU, in the full expanse that you are. In the present, you are whole. In the past, there is only a-part of you, and it is why you feel separate. In future there is only a-part of you, and it is why you feel separate. The present is the wholeness of you. It is all that created you and the possibility of you. Why would you go anywhere else?

Today, just love you. Full out love yourself. Give yourself all that you need. Do it with the commitment, understanding, and knowing that to the degree you love yourself and serve yourself, you will be able to love and serve others in the world. You are doing it for them, but it must be all about you!

Searching for life purpose? There is only one real-life purpose for all of us. It is to experience. If you are fretting over finding your purpose, you are completely missing it, because you are stagnating experience. You'll be in your purpose when you live your life on purpose.

As one door closes, another will open. As something ends, something else will begin. A new day dawns, then a night falls, bringing about another day. Everything is circular, always giving and receiving. It only stops when you hold up the natural cycle.

Close your eyes. Imagine an object of your love. Focus into your heart and allow that feeling to be magnified. Take yourself to a special moment and bask in it. Notice the sensation in your heart increase. Send those feelings that rise up love and gratitude. They are the beings that showed up to allow you to know love in all its forms. In actuality, it is you feeling love or calling for love. There is only one of us here. All things are for that one to know its Oneness.

Do not measure your worth by those around you. Do not compare what others do to what you do. We are each unique and different. Our creations will have their own unique, energetic imprint and signature. The cosmos are not complete without your unique brand of living expression. Never discount your worth, voice or creation. If you do, you are saying the Divine got it wrong. If you truly have forgotten to play, this is all going to feel frivolous, a waste of time, unnecessary and silly. But until you decide this is really here as your play, you will be working on everything. Instead, be the child at play with everything.

The child's greatest lesson is their ability to speak their truth. They are very clear and radically honest. They do not say "I think"; they say "I feel." They do not feel the need to make excuses or justify what they feel. Their words are filled with excitement and presence. They are fully attentive and speak with others, not at, above, or behind others. They are authentic and committed to play. Do not be mistaken; they are very serious about one thing: their play. It is the only thing that really matters. They came in knowing that. Their greatest gift is they show us that so clearly.

I sat in awe of Krish playing. Only a minute before, he was throwing a tantrum. As quickly as it began, it ended, because a butterfly came by. Then came the giggles. I watched in awe at the commitment to each experience and the ease with which he moved on.

The butterfly had disappeared and now he was staring at the sky, watching an airplane go by. So very excited. As it flew past, he began running through the yard with his arms spread wide apart. He was fully engaged in being the airplane, sound effects and all. I was fascinated, completely fascinated. This is what a two-year old does. This is how alive we are, how full of wonder and how care-free.

I watched my older son. I had not played in this way with him. I did not know how then. I had never been a child. I had never played. I could not connect to the sense of wonder he had, because I was not fully present to myself much less anything around me.

I thought back to how my husband and I had made him keep his voice down, how we encouraged books more than toys, how we had more indoor activities than outdoor. We did not know better. Neither of us knew what it meant to play. Neither of us had those sorts of childhoods. How could we teach what we did not know?

These children came in to teach us. I knew deeply, that was the whole reason Sage and Krish were born, to help us remember, to help us remember we came to play. We did not get the lesson with Sage, but I got it with Krish. And, hopefully, in time enough to help Sage remember play is vitally important. In fact, I realized now, it was more important than work and a greater path for manifestation and creation.

The Conduct of the Hue-Man

The culture of the new human is simple. These are people who truly walk their talk. They live that talk. They truly embody being the example of what they teach, not only a teacher talking about it. The intention is to release the baggage collected over time. Although emotional baggage is what most people think about, there are other forms. We are collectors. We collect things, lots of things. We collect people, certifications, beliefs, identities, masks, needs...and the list goes on.

There is a birthing process that occurs as one engages in this new culture. It often begins with the process of death. We must die to who we have been, what we have known, and what we hold tight to. This births us to the unknown of who we are. For most, that is a very frightening process.

As I began to feel lighter and lighter, I noticed I was becoming more sensitive to my surroundings, energetically sensitive. I was feeling and interpreting things at a much deeper level. How was this happening and why? I began looking back over my life and what I had done consistently when each level of sensitivity increased. I realized each occurrence came when I allowed myself to die. Of course, I was birthing to something in the process, but what was felt intensely was the death, the letting go of a large piece of identity. Were these identities barriers to the multi-dimensional self? It made sense. If we were locked in an identity, that part of us had limits and glass ceilings. It would carry beliefs and degrees of possibility. It would be a veil unto itself, blocking out layers of the senses. These parts that I identified with were further individuations of me, more separate parts.

While in the fashion business, my sight was focused on "seeing" beauty. It made sense that I would block greater sense perception because my mind was so caught in the work of the identity. That "me" would not even think to look beyond what I could see. As I left that career and its emotional baggage, I began seeing in an expanded sense. It was as if a curtain lifted and I could now see things I had not before, things a lot of others were not seeing.

In surrendering to being abandoned by loved ones, and especially my husband, I had to release the identity of being married, a doctor's wife, a woman that followed through on arranged marriage. I was so used to playing the roles and speaking the parts, how could I hear anything beyond those conversations? As I released those attachments and centered more in myself, I was able to hear deeper than I ever had. In that moment, I was given the guidance to begin 11:11 Magazine.

In letting go of the identity of being a retreat-center owner, coach, publisher, and teacher, I no longer had to concentrate on what I was feeling from others. I gained the ability to sense vibrations upon my skin in a deeper way, my own energy instead of taking on other's emotions. Each of these situations was a death of an identity, but it was also a birthing into more of the real me. I became aware of death not only being a part of life, but necessary to birth. Death assisted birthing to more of the living Divine. Actual physical death had to be an amazing integrative birthing to the Divine on all levels.

How could I be multi-dimensional when seeing, hearing, and feeling from a one-dimensional identity? I realized we each consciously must release our one-dimensional lives for more. We must consciously choose to continually die to who we are, in order to birth all that we do not know.

The fear comes from the ego, which is used to its routine, tasks, and control. The deeper, richer part of us naturally seeks adventure. What if you let go of everything you know, everything you "think" you know? You may open up to what you don't know, and that could lead to all kinds of amazing possibilities. Be open to completely letting go of what you "think" is reality. Life is not what you think it is. It is beyond belief!

The new human may still feel fear and trepidation of changes to come, however they look at the adventure, as opposed to the loss. There is no "real" loss for the multi-dimensional human, because only illusion can change. That which is real always remains real and true.

As I moved into continual change, I was more connected in multiple ways. I was beginning to use my senses in different capacities and on everything. Things were changing drastically. My relationships and personal possessions were changing. The nature of my work was changing. Even how I interacted with people had changed. What had not changed was my passion and compassion. My love for humanity had not changed. If anything, these realities had strengthened because I was now able to experience them in new ways.

Death is the greatest fear we have as human beings. Avoiding it drives a lot of behaviors and emotions. As we take responsibility for not only creating our reality, but being every piece and part of reality, life becomes more about living and playing in the field than dying and working the self to death. The New Dawn is awakening to the celebration that life is, embracing all of the magic that we engage with as the stuff of creation. Experiencing the brilliance of being alive in play, as play, becomes entertaining and invigorating. Emotions are truly embraced regardless of their experience, because there is an underlying joy at the gift of all of it. Even in the midst of sadness and tears, part of the multi-dimensional being is in full wonder and awareness. Internally it is awake to a conversation happening that honors the richness of the experience. It is not a thinking activity; it is full-body, integrated awareness. Every cell of one's being is alive to the sensations and emotions taking place. The entire being is in gratitude for the experience, regardless of what it is. Instead of asking "Why? Why is this happening?" this person says:

- "Yes. Feel."
- "Wow, this is the experience of crying, of deep sadness, of grief."

- "There is anger in my gut and throat, and it wants to speak. I feel it."
- "Every cell of my being feels this smile."

In the fully engaged, new human, all emotions are viewed as go(o)d emotions because they are God-being-emotion. In being true to them and embracing them, we keep the channels clear for all energy to flow. Multi-dimensional energetic beings with active multi-sensory perception are not clogged with emotional debris. They are a fully flowing system. They are the energetic structure of the Torus, a donut-shaped image where the energy is completely flowing and cycling. This is a free flowing, self-organizing, energy-generating system, when in an optimal state of being. This is how we are when we arrive. This is why children have boundless energy. Hanging onto story and not feeling emotion clogs the central channel so we tire, we age, we become cynical and serious. We become disempowered and die even before we die.

The Torus energy system that we are can be cleared, but it requires honoring all feeling, especially the fragmented bits that attempt to surface from time to time. Identifying and releasing story that has been carried is also essential. We have become hoarders of toxic material and the body homes have been filled. There is no room inside for the soul to freely live amidst the snapshots and mental news clippings. Our energy is being used up making meaning out of meaningful things, rather than engaging in a meaningful experience.

The new culture does not place meaning on things, albeit material substance or story. Meaning is experience. Wealth is not applied to how much is physically accumulated. It is the degree of experience that is allowed. This new culture of human brings about a renewed energy, reverse aging, and beautiful creative expression, all of which support communion and greater happiness.

The Vision of the Hue-Man

For the awakening human, creation will be at a whole new level. They do not feel protective of their dreams because they are the dream. They are intended to be each dream manifesting. Feeling protective or guarded would mean they are guarding themselves; that is separation.

They do not wait for an invitation; they are the invitation. They show up to serve the collective dream unfolding. They do this by being willing to be a part of another dream and have others be a part of theirs, fully understanding that as a self-organizing system, all will be served. That truth is the nature of all creation. They have an inherent knowing that there is enough and the magical mystery of the Universe has their back, if they will just have their own.

The expression of the new human is much like that of a child in belief and imagination. Possibility is not only a possibility; it is a reality to create and engage with. They begin with dreaming. This dream is brought into etheric fields by consistent language and conversation, intention and action. There is a level of focus that keeps the energy at a high. It is not forced conversation, but the childlike imaginative dreaming as if real.

Celebration and excitement are used to season the dream, drawing together necessary parts of the dream in manifestation. The dreaming must hold all kinds of thoughts, both of ease and challenge, to give it richness and depth of experience. To manifest, we must understand that we came to know the full landscape of what can occur. These elements bring it into physical reality. Commitment to the reality of it assists in birthing, even the unknown. Courage is the fuel that keeps it moving forward.

I could see that the vision of putting on a show could be reality. I imagined the set up and take down. I spoke excitedly of the experience and emotion that would be felt. In creation of the various aspects of the show, I let the full emotion of my heart come forward. I also let myself see moments where the audience size was small. I imagined pumping the gas to get from one city to the next. I let myself consider the feeling of being tired or even bored at certain parts, fully embracing those moments as well. This was to be the full-bodied experience of the unknown, but I must allow it to have some elements of what I know so that I could truly touch it in my mind and heart, in order to be able to touch it physically in this planetary reality.

Magic has nothing to do with illusion; it is all about what you are willing to see versus what you are "wanting" to see. Life works in the same way. Step out of the "want" as a place of escape. Allow yourself to be willing to create a beautiful rich story, as a means of gaining a full and expansive experience. We are each amazing storytellers, having created the experience we have already had, the ones we desire to create, and the many bubbles of time that exist, which we are completely unaware we have created.

Upon completion of Earth school, we move through a transition period where we are shown a variety of screens in holographic form. The first screen shows us the life we lived, who we touched, who we influenced, what we thought and felt. We also witness our adverse behavior: those who we treated unkindly, have hurt, or did not reconcile with. Our first task in that transition is to witness ourselves as we really were and others as they really were, without all the perceptions and projections.

As we move to other screens, we see all the possibilities that the life had, because in some bubble they were played out. While alive, many of us have wondered what would have happened had a different choice been made. In the holographic replay, we see those alternate paths. Physical experience was limited by what you believed possible and where you let the imagination roam. The hologram illustrates that all was possible from the greater mind and plays out the full imagination.

Children do that when they are naturally playing. They will speak of the many scenarios of a situation with excitement and wonder. The child plays this out in their imaginations and inherently knows the ability to play this out as reality. But, the world places time and limits on the ways of the child. What could you have that you have not allowed as possible, because you do not take the time to imagine and dream? What current reality is in place simply because you have not placed innocent wondering eyes upon it?

The new human understands that many bubbles of reality exist and is utilizing voice, mind, and heart to tap into a particular bubble. This translates in the practical sense into language, thoughts, and feelings, aligned and focused. This creative manipulation of energy brings forward the elements necessary to have the experience. There is nothing impossible. If it is your desire to meet a particular person, it is only possible if you truly believe it is possible. It will only happen if you hold the focus, excitement, and play of it happening. Time will be rewoven to match up to that bubble of reality.

This can be done with anything: a life partner, a personal aspiration, a global solution. Focusing upon that desire creates the vibration that brings together, in a self-organizing way, the individuals who would resonate and align in the highest order. This collective group of people will hold a frequency that is linked, as a crystalline structure of community forms to bring about the reality of that intention. This also occurs because there are many other parts of you desiring the same thing.

Imagine how a snowflake begins. It starts as a molecule of water that freezes. It builds, collecting other molecules, creating a unique design. This intricate and beautiful structure will be a design like no other, locking into place the specific crystalline molecules that manifest a uniquely beautiful design. It holds a frequency and a vibration. Just as Masuru Emoto's research has illustrated, frequency can be imprinted upon the water. What are we but mostly water? As we connect, the collective water will hold a certain frequency.

Mind you, there is no good or bad. There is, however, a range of frequency. It is not that others do not appear along the way. After all, this is Earth school. The curriculum involves discernment, learning, and growing. This is not to judge others that come along, but to consciously choose what stays in the manifestation. Regardless of what shows up, it is the initial dreamer. If it is not desirable, it is appearing so that you clear it out internally. This is how you clarify the field so you manifest the highest expression of what is trying to form. It also requires the elements of language, culture, and vision to focus in staying the course. Choice is always the most important element of creation.

The beauty of this experience is co-creation with the Self, the many pieces and parts appearing as others. You bring the best of what you do, they bring the best of what they do, and music is created. It becomes a symphony of sound as more voices become involved. It is not orchestrated; it is not planned. It is the natural law of the Universe, your Universe, for like to attract that which it is like. The best encounters arise as accidents, as do the most amazing creations. At the end of the day, we are all artists, strokes of the Creator. What makes beautiful art is not the appearance of the painting in the end; it is the heart and belief of that creator knowing his power to paint the canvas. Do you know your power in the canvas you paint? Certainty is the pathway for spontaneous evolution and unfolding possibility. The Divine Path has always existed. It is finally living, being, and knowing this Divine Path. Many have wandered off course, but you may "wonder" back.

We are the neurological network for Gaia. The reason that the planet is illustrating weather patterns and biological patterns of upheaval and collapse is because we are the network that keeps all the programming in place. We believe a neurological network is a beneficial thing. We believe the thinking and computing capacity is a necessity to sustain this human neuro-network that is in place. But, this is the very brain that is creating the play in the forces of nature. Gaia is responding to the repetitive thoughts and embedded programming of pain that exists within this neurological network. What is coming back to us in the ways of weather patterns and catastrophic occurrences is Gaia's response to the programming. If we are a society holding the code, then the output must be the code.

In a neurological network, there is input programming and output programming. The factor that has not been focused on, but quite present and valuable, is the unknown between those two. We have been operating, creating, and connecting by what has been put in. We have yet to fully tap into the "unknown" of the network. When we do so, we will advance creative capacity, engage in full multi-sensory connection, and align with the earth's grid system and the Divine plan. We need only get with the program and the programming. The problem with the neurological program is that it is logical. We must go beyond logic, beyond the brain, and dive into that we cannot physically see, feel, hear, and touch. This greater intelligence is a self-created awakening that opens the vast portals lying deeply within our cellular structure. We are a mass of Universes. Just diving into the void in one space, we will know the expansiveness of all space. In no time, we discover that the truth of the God-code was on the inside, never on the outside.

The entire Universe is based on a binary coding of 1 and 0. 1 symbolizes oneness and 0 indicates the void. The human mind would view oneness as what is desired and 0, the void, as nothingness. In actuality, the 0 is the unknown possibility. The 1 is the oneness but it is also what we know, in its full spectrum of polarity. The 1 is the input and the output. The 0, or "void," is the unknown factor to be discovered that aligns us with the Gaia grid system and Divine plan. The Divine plan is the universal programming. We are one file system among many, running its programs. To expand beyond the programming, we must engage with and become the vision of the void. The vision of the new human is the willingness to dive into the black hole and be the Light within it. This will arise through the full expanse of experience experiencing itself unharnessed, in full sensory spontaneous being. That will be the spontaneous healing so many are seeking. As we dive into the void, we activate within each cell the unknown capacity it holds. We initiate an awakening in the DNA structure, a sequence of openings that bring together the senses and God-energy into integration and full illumination. The unknown of the Self becomes illuminated. This has been the missing link to our truth expression.

My heart kept waking to one feeling. "I know who I am from what I have lived through. I have defined myself by what has wounded me and the things that have helped me grow. I have created based on what I have been exposed to. I have limited myself by what I know. Who am I beyond this? What way may I be defined beyond the stories I have told myself, or that others have told me about me? What have I not created that is possible? What if I were to have no limits?" The words kept reverberating in my head. My desire had been in seeking to be whole. I then moved to desiring to experience Oneness. Then, what? What was beyond the experience of Oneness? This was the void, the unknown. I realized what I had really always been seeking was to discover my unknown self, the part of me that extended beyond every story, belief, achievement, creation, ego, mind, body, heart, and soul. Who...what...when... where...how was that?

I don't know what I am doing....

I don't know how I am going to do it....

I don't know where it is leading....

I don't know why it is happening....

I don't know who I am becoming....

In this moment, I don't need to know.

In this moment, I desire to un-know.

I am willing to dive into the Great Unknown as I die to the known self.

Take my oneness into the void that I discover my allness.

The Awakening of the Lightness: An Activation

The laughter is felt deep, incorporating every cell, free and unguarded in nature. This embrace sees life as it is, not as we want it to be, but as an amazing creation that need not be shied away from, lest we desire to be coy with our own Self. It is my lighthearted desire and intention to fully embody...

Living in devotion to my authentic soul nature.

Intimacy with my dreams, desires, and creative capacity.

Beauty of self-expression and soulful creation.

Epiphanies and synchronicities as a direct conversation with my Universe.

Resource fullness as a way to expand the experience of ease.

Art fullness as an understanding of my unique creative capacity.

Truth.

Impeccability.

Oneness into the void.

Now in no-time.

Play in the Light of Transparency

I
want to
play with you.
Ups and downs!
Where they go, nobody knows!
I am tall, I am small, I am narrow, I am wide. Who Am I?
You birthed as a Divine AHA moment.
A sacred giggle had you BE.
In the lightness of Love,
All of Creation had a moment where
Love fell in Love with the thought of you.
A stroke of insight and a splash of color
The casting of flesh created one like no other.
Divinely designed spiritual technology
Engaging sacred entertainment.
A Divine comedy, A Divine tragedy
Stories layered upon one another,
The great novel of the Universe
Spanning all space and time.
Epic, Uber, Legendary
Written in the stars eons ago
WE have forgotten to play.
We have forgotten *how* to play.
It is time to remember.
Will you play
with
me
?

Transparency removes all of the obstacles from seeing clearly. Seeing will occur either way, because even the obstacles bear gifts that ultimately lead us to places of clarity. But willingly being transparent lifts the weight of the world off the shoulders so that there is a feeling of Lightness. Transparency would mean looking into our own lives through a clear pane of glass, as the experience of play, instead of gazing through the pain of a story we desire to make an ongoing reality. The latter is the road to seriousness, the greatest disease on the planet. Lightness through transparency allows freedom and power to reign, because there is no longer shame, blame, or judgment. The mere act of transparency releases life from all that would bind it. This reveals the ladder inside of us interweaving oneness and the void, both of which have been inside all along.

See-Saw: Ups and Downs!

Do you remember being on a see-saw? Up and down...up and down...up and down. It was always amazing to go high in the sky and then come down with a thump! In those moments, on the way up and on the way down, it was not about the top or the bottom, it was always about flying through the air. It was flying, being weightless, not having a care in the world.

Life is much like a see-saw: going high, reaching for the top, and coming down with a thump! We tend to focus on the "thump" as we get older. Or we are always focused on reaching the top and completely forgot to enjoy the experience in between. The in-between is the really good part. That is the journey. As experience experiencing itself, meaning is found in the middle, between the ups and the downs of life. Don't get so caught up in the highs and lows; they are just a part of the ride—they are not the full ride!

Select three life experiences in your life that had both a high and low. Focus on the journey in between those two points, both going up and coming down.

- How were you in those experiences?
- What beautiful nuggets did they add to life?
- How can you look at these now and be a little less serious about it all?
- Can you allow life to be a varied composition of experiences that see-saw?

Around the Carousel: Where They Go, Nobody Knows!

Do you know the interesting thing about carousels? They always bring you back to where you were. They take you up and down and all around, but you will come back to where you were in the beginning.

Life and its experiences are that merry-go-round. Your choices and circumstances will take you up and down and all around for the sake for bringing you back to the beginning—your beginning. You knew something when you first got on this merry-go-round. You knew who you were and how to play where you were. And then you didn't. No worries! Life kept bringing you back so you could remember.

- What is this carousel—filled with lions, tigers, and bears—called life, continually bringing you back to?
- What areas of your life do you find yourself constantly going in circles because you do not stop the carousel?

- Are you changing positions on your merry-go-round to get a different perspective each time?

Hall of Mirrors: I Am Tall, I Am Small, I Am Narrow, I Am Wide...Who Am I? I AM

Did you ever go into one of those hall of mirrors and see how you changed and contorted? In some places, you were stretched; in others, you were pulled. Some left gaping holes in you; some made you swell. Others were scary, quite a few were funny, but all of them were you. That never changed. Your appearance changed. Your experience of yourself changed, but what was inherent within you could not change regardless of what mirror appeared.

Funny how life operates in the same way. People show up in our lives to show us who we are being, as do circumstances. The people that appear will let us see the many faces we wear, our behaviors, and our judgments. Some are scary, others powerful; some are wounded and others happy. But in the end, it is all you and will bring you back to center. The circumstances in life are mirrors as well. As we reflect upon those, it is apparent there have been many moments of being stretched, pulled, and contorted. In the end, regardless of what the mirrors show us, it is a carousel. We are to develop good attitudes, know we have a choice to change positions in any moment, and go around as many times as it takes before we decide to get off the ride. All the while, lovely music accompanies us. Mirror, Mirror, what say you?

- What mirrors continually appear in your life so you gain clarity on who you are being?

- Can you celebrate three experiences that have stretched and pulled you to see a different reflection of yourself?

- What attitude do you maintain through life? Is it a merry one?

I am the one who sees.

I am the eye, the I, of the Universe, a Divine ONE.

My vision shines upon the world.

I am the Divine Imagination who paints a world that isn't.

I am Divine Illustration who draws out magnificent works of art.

I am the Divine Sculptor producing great symmetry, forming Master Pieces into Master Peace.

I am the Divine Canvas upon which to begin.

I cast the line that initiates a grand design.

I am the clay. I am the water.

I am the potter. I am the fire.

I am the clay pot.

I am the beautiful gift.

I am that which has yet to fill the container.

I am the space of the unknown...waiting to become known.

The truth is out!

THE INITIATION

Every situation in life has been an initiation—the leap forward, an activation; the reconciliation and clearing, the integration; and all of it leads to the brilliance of your illumination. Let each moment in life be an awakening to some untapped part of you. This is not just time passing by. It is all with purpose. You need only conduct your life on purpose, committed to fully experiencing each moment.

We are not to wait for something to happen. A moment or event is not to happen to you. You are to happen to the event or moment. There have been so many times when people were in anticipation of an event or set of dates, waiting for something big to occur that would change everything...an eclipse, the full moon, a meteor, 11-11-11, 12-12-12, or 12-21-12. Of course, these were or are heightened times for energy and openings. But where do you think they occur? These were not to tap you on the shoulder, suddenly changing anything and everything. They are markers—messages in fact. They are symbolic of a time to open. These things occur inside of you. But as in most cases, we have become lazy and unconscious. There is no quick fix. That is not why we have come. We have come to play full out. It is time to stop gazing up at the stars and instead become the stars.

We are the gateways, the locks and the keys. We are the strings and the strands. We are the hypothesis and the theory. We are the ones we have been waiting for. Willingness to step forward, and be that experience, engages the opening.

We are initiated through experience, both the challenging and the easy. It is in the more challenging experiences that initiation occurs. On a deep cellular level, within the DNA strands, there are locks and keys. Specific leaps of consciousness are keys to scaling the great ladder that rests within. Having the courage to be the change leads to the deeper treasures that have been hidden away. The secret garden, this heaven, lay within you.

You are comprised of God-stuff. This mystical essence is a series of locks and keys, each opening with your alignment to the truth of who you are. There is an energetic opening that happens each time we choose to move from a lower vibration of thought and action to the next level. Conscious choice and response are the graduation of the soul as it awakens to the unknown of itself.

Awareness, the byproduct of growth, is relative and personal. The one who believes she is most aware usually has much to discover. The ONE who is truly aware realizes he knows nothing. This ONE, rather than proclaiming enlightenment, will live life being the light, being the change. In doing so, this individual taps into a magical sphere of co-creation. This is a realm any can attain. If a person is willing to walk the narrow path of moment-by-moment courageous living, in an expression of openness and vulnerability, then mystical life is a continuous experience, while all others live what is currently normality.

Initiation is not something you feel, but you will see it. How? There will be a series of events that begin as goodness and synchronicity. This is how you know you are awakening to another bubble of reality. It is how you realize you are emerging from the chrysalis to a new form. In actuality, it is the cellular structure morphing to a new state of being. On the inside, it appears as if a butterfly dives back into a cocoon. The cocoon is a sacred space. It is stillness, quietness, and meditative. It is the place of power where the ONE eventually emerges, gaining courage and commitment to burst through.

Most people love the idea of being the emerged butterfly. They can't wait to leave the chrysalis. However, the true nutrients for change and evolution rest within encasement of the cocoon.

The emerged butterfly is new life, excitement, and joy. It quickly forgets its encasement. As the butterfly, we fly, but we begin seeking nutrients on the outside. The world is enamoring. This emergence is another opportunity to become blinded by the beauty of what we see in the outside world. The butterfly moves from beautiful flower to flower, but its true evolution was gained pushing through.

In each step of awakening, you will encounter a new world, because you are a new person. You experience the world from a new perspective. Your attraction factor is going to bring you new interactions and experiences. The world will appear with a different shimmer, as new baubles and sparkly objects show up in terms of experiences, people, and things. Each phase is a test as to whether you can remain committed to what is real or become mesmerized by the illusion. Even the most "enlightened" person can fall victim to their new experience of the world, as they once again find themselves off course. But, even that is alright; this too is experience.

The outer world is the place of course correction, hence why it is termed Earth school. This play on the outside is designed so that we are led back inside when necessary. However, the outer world has become so enamoring, we are forgetting the importance of the quiet inner world. Everything from personal turmoil to weather patterns is creating course correction. It is not God doing this to us. It is our own intelligence, individual and collective, balancing the outer focus back inside. We are not to become hermits, but a certain degree of introspection is necessary to create renewed balance in the world. Inner reflection helps awareness and innate intelligence arise.

We are to always keep one eye/I on the inside while the other eye/I is playing on the outside. The third eye/I is the space between that can tap into the unknown. This is the trinity of full experience.

The Universe is naturally realigning us, always shaping us towards the ultimate Divine Plan. In the past, it was called the "dark night of the soul." However, there is a radical difference now. The dark night was a breaking down of life, a belief in pain and brokenness. The evolved human has a different approach, a much more proactive one.

When course correction happens, where does the more conscious person go? They return inside, back into the quiet solace of the interior landscape. It is not an escape method, like depression or isolation. This is the willingness to contemplate and witness oneself. We are learning to view the experience, replaying the hologram in the mind now, rather than waiting for the reconciliation of life after crossing over to the other side. The new human is not interested in the story created. She seeks growth and awareness. There is a deeper level of self-love and personal commitment to experiencing. There is no place for blame, because there is no one to blame. There is no one else in this virtue-all reality. There is only one of us here; it is you.

Is this an evolutionary experience? Yes and no. The evolution is externally measured but only accomplished through constant involution. There really is not anything "out there." It is only a projection of what is "in here." The body is the cocoon. In each new emergence, we are a newly beginning stage of growth. If we let each new level be infancy, with complete forgetting as initial birth, creation and expansion occur in an unencumbered way. What this means is to begin every phase from a clean and clear perspective, without identity or filters.

In the past, we have unconsciously brought forward memory, baggage, and filters. With each new initiation, we leave those pieces, because there is more interest in looking deep inside rather than looking back. The past is no longer the story we drag around; it is honored as a beginning point for the creation of each individual. The more evolved human celebrates the past, especially the challenge, as ground zero, the foundational place of initiation. These are initiations of Light, not stages of darkness. We have always been connected, having Light continually pumped into our bodies from our Source.

In holding conscious awareness of the eye/I on the inner, outer, and unknown landscapes of multi-dimensionality, new methods of strengthening light quotients can be held. In moving into a multisensory life, we utilize all of the senses in new ways to strengthen our bodies of Light. By stretching the ways the senses are used, the world can be experienced multi-dimensionally.

At birth, the umbilical cord is cut. It is the source of life and nutrients for the fetus. It is also the source of Light and nurturance from Source, but this occurs on more than a physical level. We may have had our umbilical cords cut, but the energetic version of that has remained all along. However, we have not been taught of this connection. It is not only your connection; you are that.

Imagine this line of Light on the front of your spine. This is the place to maintain your focus. Place every dream, intention, and desire within this line of Light, so that it is nurtured by the Divine Presence that is. Consciously bring into your awareness the energetic umbilical cord that continually nourishes you from the unseen realms. This cord is hooked in to your hara line, always feeding you with the Divine Light connection. Think of an astronaut in space. He maintains a connection to the shuttle through a connection cord, never really leaving the shuttle but moving out in space.

You are Divinity. You have always been. Life's experiences occur to bring you to that remembrance. There is no need to look for truth. There is no need to find it. You never lost it. It is inside of you. When the questions come, listen within; the answer will follow.

- Where am I? *I AM EVERYWHERE.*
- What am I? *I AM EVERYTHING.*
- Who am I? *I AM ALL THAT IS.*
- How am I? *I AM ALWAYS PERFECTION UNFOLDING.*
- Why am I? *I AM EXPERIENCE AND CREATION EXPRESSING ITSELF.*
- When? *ALWAYS IN ALL WAYS.*

An essence exists inside of you, a rich Divine Essence. Not only is it inside of you, it is you. It is pure being. This original form is the concentrate from which we come. It's the juice—succulent, refreshing, nourishing, sparkling power! We came from Divine Source, as smaller individuations of it. This flows within us, from us, and around us. It is also what we marinate in all of the time. We cannot get away from it. It can never leave us. You are God-stuff.

This essence that you are is a Divine inheritance. It is why you are a Master and always have been, whether or not you recognize or act upon that truth. You are, in essence, equal to all Masters. There are twelve sovereigns in alignment with the throne of Divinity. These encompass the crowning glories of the Kingdom that we are originally born with. However, we strip ourselves of these by choosing distortions over Light.

We are Love; this is an eternal ever-expanding truth. Fear is a choice, as is lack, limitation, and disempowered living. As ruler of your Kingdom, your command is always adhered to. You can have what you want; just choose those things that serve you well.

The Essence that we are never leaves us. The twelve sovereigns are freedoms we possess and may reclaim. We may choose sovereignty in any moment. When we choose to live as the Divine Children of the Universe on the vast playground of creation, we open to receive all of the riches of the Kingdom. The issue is not that we have become separate from; that is not possible. The primary issue is that we have forgotten how to play.

Many are trying to remember or return to who they really are. This is being identified as many things: authentic power, presence, energy, spirit, and so on. Yes, you are all these things, but more. Those are aspects of you. The irony is that you are being who you really are whether you know it or not, conscious of it or not, acting intentionally or not.

Creation happens because you are that.

You are creation, creating itself.
You are the experience of creation, experiencing itself.
Your remembrance is that you are.
You always have been the Divine Essence of Creation.
You are the power and presence of Creation.
Consider all that has been created as you remember this.
Consider the vastness of creation as you remember this.
Consider all time as you remember this.
Consider all power as you remember this.
Consider all knowing as you remember this.
Consider all that you are, have been, and can become.

The Essence of Divine Wonder

Blowing bubbles with your lips...trying to catch a butterfly...running with a superhero cape...being mesmerized by a caterpillar... sticking out your tongue to taste the snow...collecting acorns...flying a kite...building sandcastles at the beach...

There is a space of innocence, openness, and playfulness that exists as our natural knowing. These innate natures are activated when we engage with life from the essence of wonder. Within each object and person we meet exists two parts, the known and the unknown. Past experience illustrates the human condition of responding and reacting from what is known. We react from our known filters, which distort the experience. Then, we add what we know about the person or thing; we add perception.

What if you began everything on a clean slate? What if you knew nothing and allowed yourself to see everything with fresh eyes? What if we could view the world with the wonder-full eyes of a child? The complete agenda of a three-year-old is to play. Everything is something to touch, taste, feel, and know. Each moment and encounter are one and the same. They are a combination of presence and imagination. They are "a-live" experience. Their aliveness is the foundation of wonder. They maintain that state of being, the aliveness of discovery. Wonder is the constant state of meeting the Divine in another form.

Wonder is more than being enthralled at something. It relates to true intimacy, something the world has gotten away from. For a child, wonder and intimacy are synonymous. Children connect completely with whatever they are engaged with. Whether it is a toy, an animal, insect, activity, or person, the child dives fully into it. They embrace everything with fullness, desiring to be wholly immersed in oneness. For the child, everything is holy, a sacred meditation. They do not know this, because they are being it instead of doing it. A child would not call it that, but watch them. They are completely present, with full mind but not in the mind. They are the greatest example of living meditation.

We have come to believe in the sterile, seriousness of meditation. For adults, it has a purpose or the individual is seeking a result. It has time set aside or has become ritual. True meditation happens without planning it, in fact, without the intense focus. True meditation is mindless. It is play and connection. Meditation is really not so much about stillness as it is engagement, wholehearted engagement. This place of discovery holds reverence for what can be known in a new way.

It is wonder, and in this place, there is no wandering. Why? The mind cannot wander because it is not in charge. It is involved, rather than being preoccupied with being evolved. Here the mind may receive. It is not processing, inputting, or directing. It is not thinking, but instead, it is open to awareness. The mind engages from the place of the unknown, even if somewhere in its filing system, it has the answers.

Wonder is the moving droplet of discovery. Children do not identify who they are and then participate. They leave out the "I" when immersed. If another toy or activity comes along, they simply move their awareness. In an instant, their focus is on something else, and they are one with that. They have left the other, completely detaching from it and beginning the process of discovery again.

Adults do not do this. We either have to finish one thing and begin another, deciding we will go back at some point, or file some information to hang on to. When we engage in something new, rather than being open to the newness, we come in with what we know and attempt to place that knowing upon the very thing we don't know. That is neither engagement, nor discovery; it is force and control. This behavior is about the "I," the smaller version of the self, and its need to know it knows.

Divine Wonder is the aspect of the Divine Child that has no need to know, no need to define, control, manipulate, or force. The Divine Child is present as pure experience and awareness. The Divine Child does not say, "I must work with this to evolve." Without thinking, he moves into play with it and involves himself. Wonder stems from a deep knowing of being "in the world but not of it." Divine Wonder is being in the world and playing in the discovery of what has been created, the world you have created, the world that is you.

The Essence of Divine Wisdom

Believe and it will happen. You can do whatever you want, but you willingly give that up. God does not want us to hate. The trees talk, but you have to listen. There are golden lights all around us. Our bodies are musical instruments.

My heart told me. What does your heart say?

Children do not hesitate speaking their truth. They are fully connected to their bodies and feelings, coming in with the understanding of sensations and verbalizing those. In this way, they state what they feel, as the overseer of the body vehicle they inhabit. They do not know this on an intellectual level; they live from a place of deep intelligence. This is Divine Wisdom.

Children speak from a humble place, a place of depth. The wise overseer of this physical body is also an overseer of the life that surrounds it. Children witness life in wonder, both engaged and involved. They are clear and forgiving. They are love, complete unconditional Love. These elements allow them to be open for connection in both the inner and outer realms of experience. They embrace everything without judgment or bias. They channel divine messages in simplicity.

This level of open connection is what brings truth through the channels of the body. It is felt, heard, seen, and touched. They are completely empathic, soaking in everything on many levels. The child bears witness to all, utilizing all senses in full capacity to know that truth. This is why it comes so clearly through them. There are no filters. They are not guarded, because they have not yet been conditioned to be less than they are. In being uninhibited and free, they are truth purveyors: "out of the mouths of babes...."

Children do not learn the truths they speak. They simply state them. There is no attachment. They are connecting what speaks internally to what is speaking externally, and providing the words to balance these worlds. In the moments such wisdom comes, it is because they innately sense the discordance of the two worlds and they know they are harmony. They are being that balancing harmony. Children come in as that bridge. They are clear channels. They speak without hindrance in saying what comes to them.

As adults, we call it Higher Wisdom, but again that indicates it is above or outside. Adults value the wisdom that comes from experience. They forget to trust the wisdom that is inherent. We have come to believe in the outer experience, giving it more value. It is why we have to work for our wisdom. It is why there is necessity in creating peaks and valleys to traverse. We have forgotten how to be the bridge between two worlds. If there were no attachment to either world, nor the veils attained over time, clarity would come easily. Adults can once again become clear channels of Divine Wisdom by allowing the Divine Child to reawaken.

Divine Wisdom is the place of non-identity. There is no point in expressing who "I" am because you are one with all of it. Children are masters at manifesting, because their consciousness rests in this space. They do not come in with an ego; their filters and surroundings create the ego.

For children, the truth is spoken calmly and quickly. Then, they are immediately engaged in the next experience. There is no need for discussion. There is no attempt to think about it. They do not go into the mind for different options. They are fully functioning from the heart space. The Divine Wisdom of a child is not of the mind. Children are in-the-moment experience.

- Who were you before you decided who you were?
- How was life before you took on the beliefs and feelings of those around you?
- What did you see, hear, feel, and know before you were told it was not real?
- When truth comes through you, do you feel the present, but detached, nature of it?
- When has your wisdom come from experience versus knowing?
- In what "play" does the mind step out of the way and intelligence come shine through?

The Essence of Divine Confidence

- Who loves you? *God loves me.*
- Who else loves you? *I love me.*
- Who else loves you? *Mommy loves me.*
- Who else loves you? *Daddy loves me.*
- Who else loves you? *My friends love me.*
- Who else loves you? *Everybody loves me.*

Confidence builds after doing something again and again. It encompasses building a muscle of self-belief, which usually has extended arms of self-esteem and self-love, although those can be in varying degrees. Confidence, from the human perspective, involves trusting the self and a certain level of trust in the world. However, due to filters, we can only trust the world to the degree the self is trusted.

Children come into the world trusting. They are born without fears. Divine Confidence is complete trust, knowing that everything is always happening in the best interest of one's life. There is no question or judgment. Because there is no worry, the future is not an issue. The present is always perfect, because each moment holds both the magic and the teaching.

Children manifest naturally because of this reliance on life. They come in knowing life will provide the needs required. As this is confirmed, they engage fully, innately utilizing the sovereign essences, which continue to prove that the world can be trusted.

Play without agenda or attachment results in the law of attraction in its highest sense. A child does not need to know the law of attraction, create vision boards, or state affirmations. They do not need to write million-dollar checks, or sit and hold visualizations. Why? Because, they do not hold the energy of doing; they are the energy of being. This is the highest expression of all the laws. It naturally creates attraction.

A child does not plan a vision board but may continually draw pictures of bicycles or fish. In that excitement and continual focus, a bicycle or aquarium will manifest. With that said, the physical item is not really important to the child. They are not attached to it. They are whole-heartedly engaged in the celebration of their experience and the expansive realism of the imagination as a playground. Their illusion has become reality just as easily as many of our realities are truly illusions. This is why their manifestations move from the energetic plane to the physical plane at a faster rate.

Children are engaged and filled with a deep level of trust. We have forgotten how to trust. We do not want to surrender to something beyond our control. The irony is that we are always guiding life and being guided. We either guide creation from the small self or from the fullness of the God-self. In turn, guidance will support whichever we choose.

When surrendering to the Divine plan, we manifest what we most desire from the very depths of our soul. This does not always match what our conscious mind believes it needs. The grown-up personality wants what it wants, mostly out of a place of distrust and fear. It chooses based on the status quo and having fallen victim to what society has portrayed as the successful life. Grown-ups want what they believe they need, rather than trusting the field that surrounds them.

When living from a place of Divine Confidence, the individual possesses the no-fear attitude that we witness in children. These people embrace challenges from a deep understanding that obstacles will move. This foundation of confidence unlocks potential and possibility as the individual takes on each new moment, weaving together the warp and woof in the fabric of reality. Exerting mastery in every scenario is natural because these people are steeped in the knowing that the Universe has their back. Conversations with the Universe continually happen as the signs and symbols of direction.

The Essence of Divine Curiosity

It feels squishy. It smells funny. It looks strange. It is so cute. I bet it tastes sour. Touch it. I want to taste it. Shhhh. Listen. Do you hear that?

The essence of Divine Curiosity is opening to everything in life with excitement. We are endowed with senses that go unused, for the most part. These senses were given to us for the celebration of creation. Everything created is multisensory and can be experienced in multisensory ways. We have limited ourselves, and creation, by minimizing these gifts.

We minimize the excitement of everything around us by not fully taking everything in or expressing it outwardly. When a person thinks of the breath, the inhale and the exhale, focus is on the lungs. For someone more aware, there is acknowledgment that the nose or the mouth are also involved. Someone in greater awareness may realize other body parts are involved or moving.

However, someone in true celebration of the breath and all of life might see that we are not breathing at all, but are the ones being breathed. What if life is actually exhaling and inhaling into us? What if we are really what we believe the lungs to be? What if we are part of a greater body? All of a sudden, the mystery begs curiosity, and this becomes excitement and play.

The same thing happens every time we have an AHA moment. Curiosity is peaked. Something is celebrated, and another part of us, the creative capacity, becomes enthralled to know more. For a brief moment, perhaps longer, it is simply pure awareness.

As we enter the human experience, we come in as explorers. Babies look around with curiosity. They can sense when Mom is near by her smell. Everything goes into the mouth. They fully take in what they encounter, becoming connected as they explore. In doing this, a more authentic life experience occurs because there is a sense of freedom and connection in many ways.

Think of a baby that has just discovered their hands. They look in wonder and surprise. The fingers and fists go to the mouth. They move about excitedly, interacting with the hand as if in communion. Notice how we take our hands for granted.

Now, think about a baby's feet. The big toe ends up in the mouth; the ankles are hugged to the chest. All of a sudden the whole foot is far over the head. Curiosity begets connection, which turns into play and becomes experience. There is an innate Divine Curiosity to discover and know everything around us.

Most things on Earth can be explored in a multitude of ways. When we do not allow ourselves to unlock curiosity, there is no way to celebrate the person, place, or thing on the outside. By understanding what is out there, we are better able to have curiosity about ourselves. Everything is a mirror, an aspect of yourself here to show you...you.

What if being curious about things actually provides answers about you? Everything is indeed you. Don't you desire to know yourself, discover another aspect, or encounter a piece you have never seen before? When you embark on everything with this Divine Curiosity, you open to other aspects of the self, which expand the awareness and activation within the cells.

It is not to say we should eat mud or touch fire, but is this not what children do? They are curious, and things will be smelled, tasted, touched, and felt. This integrates the experience on a deeper level. You may not desire to take in a spoonful of mud, but let all of your senses awaken to it. Let curiosity play. How curious this thing called mud! Squish it between your toes, smell it up your nose, pour it down your back to see how it flows, speak to it and see what it knows. Pat it and bake it. Just celebrate and play with it!

In every moment, we have a choice to become excited about life or pass by it. If we take a moment to truly celebrate every magnificent creation, this becomes a very magical place. Instead of focusing on stories, we can become part of the scenery that is begging to be seen, touched, tasted, and smelled. Every item has the ability to be experienced through all of the senses, which creates a multitude of ways to express Divine Curiosity.

Curiosity may be expressed with the body. It can also be experienced in the imagination or in the breath. In the same way, everything out there can be experienced through sight, smell, taste, sound, touch, intuition, and humor. These are your senses and they are tools for the essence of Divine Curiosity. The more you engage multiple senses into every experience, the deeper you will experience multi-sensory living. Encountering life, in this way, lifts various veils of perception because you release the limits on powerful tools you possess.

Celebrate everything in life with excitement. Allow curiosity to assist you in connecting to the world. You will discover it results in a deeper connection to the Greater Self and multiple layers of the inner world. Instead of having an AHA moment once in a while, be curious enough to allow every moment to become an ongoing ecstatic AHHHHH.

The Essence of Divine Impulse

Triple-decker ice cream sundaes! Let's go to the beach! Pitch a tent tonight? Want to build a tunnel with sheets and pillows? First one to the top wins!

The energies of spontaneity and passion create open doors of opportunity, synchronistic encounters, and meetings of powerful influence. The impact of energy is so magnetic that it acts like a lightning rod, bringing about that which is highly energized like itself. When this occurs, it may look like lucky breaks or miracles, but it is far beyond that. It is the immersion into life as aliveness. If it can be sustained, it creates a direct path to the highest possibility.

Divine Impulse is the desire to dance through life, not walk; to leap, not skip; to laugh, not smile. It is the romantic longing of life to taste the tears one cries, to hear words of love with the poet's heart, or to know bliss as both lover and beloved. Divine Impulse is not simply in the moment; it is all of the movement within the moment, by living out the emotion in every cell. This embodiment brings experience in full embrace of the feeling, regardless of whether it is anguish, rage, bliss, or love. All senses are immersed, all emotions cherished. Thoughts and imagination also marinate within the expanse of emotion experienced. There is no fear in creating something undesirable, because letting the mind touch all bubbles of reality keeps us from suppressing thoughts into the subconscious. It is the subconscious thoughts that generally wreak havoc on our lives. By embracing all possibilities, we free our lives from unconscious turns of "fate."

The experience is not held or carried. It is felt only as long as the experience lasts, and then it washes through. From here, the next spontaneous moment is immersed in. Change takes place as a continual building and tearing down. Energy is placed wherever the whim is. This is not haphazard or chaotic. It is consciousness of overall experience, but indulges in the spontaneity being asked for in that moment.

Children do this exquisitely. In play, they build towers to tear them down. They put together puzzles and then take them apart. They engage in this continuous play out of excitement and the ability to create again and again. They know they are a never ending well of ideas and creation. They never feel as if they lose by tearing down what was built, because what can come will only be better. For a child, there is only increase. They will also add in new elements. Divine Impulse creates through expansion and connection. When the thought arises, a child simply acts. They are a constant YES for creation. They never question; they just move.

We receive divine impulses all of the time. However, as adults, we do not always follow through. We stop at every impulse and choose to be practical or analyze it. This is how we create a slowdown in manifestation and synchronicity. By hesitating or pausing, we step out of the way of the Divine Plan so what would naturally occur still does; we are just not in the way of it to happen for us.

What if everything in your life was simply a YES? Had you lived in the constant YES from childhood, how different would your life be? How different would you be? When we follow Divine Impulse, we are engaged in experience. There is no room for regret, because we followed the calling of the heart. Note, I said calling of the heart. The Divine Impulse always comes through the heart and will be felt deep in the gut. It will never come from the mind.

Hesitation may cause regret. More often, people hold regret because they did not do something. They did not give into the YES. The impulses that come from the mind will typically be the deceptive ego at play. You will know when this happens because you will go back and forth about an idea. There will be worry and the desire to discuss it with many, still not sure of the decision. This is not Divine Impulse; it is manipulation of matter. However, even if you choose to say YES to the head, there is never a mistake because it is all experience. In the midst of a mental choice, the heart will always find a way through, allowing Divine Impulse to strike even then. There is a Divine Plan, and regardless of how we tend to veer off, there is not a moment where we are not given the impulses to set us back on course.

What does that have to do with the impulse to build a triple-decker sundae or race to the top of a hill on a whim? Our ability to say YES builds the muscle for spontaneous action. As we learn this conversation with the Essence that is, the world aligns itself with our movement. A rhythm and pace is established to match up with our movements.

The Essence of Divine Humor

Let's pretend! You be the bad guy! Pretend I am stuck in quicksand.

Yeah, I'll be trapped and have to find my way out. I'll figure out a way and be a hero!

The greatest issue with the world in this moment is seriousness. This dis-ease is controlling and killing humanity. Seriousness stems from an inability to relax into life. It is fighting without a true intent or purpose. We have lost sight of the prize: ourselves. All of a sudden, the world has become more important to us than ourselves.

We bought into the idea of survival and struggle. We believe that life is about the fight. To affirm these beliefs and in homage to the ancestors that lived this life, we have followed suit. It is ingrained in us early on. We begin as young children, concocting stories of tragedy and triumph. Little boys play war with their Lego pieces. Little girls create drama in the dollhouse. How do we know of struggle from such a young age other than being taught that it is a way of life?

Children appear before us continually fabricating realities. What an amazing message they bring. Do we not continuously fabricate reality? If we have been given this ability, why not create what we truly want? We do have experiences that are going to tug on the heart and bring in waves of deep emotion, but we must step back from time to time and remember we created the whole thing.

The humor of it all is that we seriously believe our stories, when in fact we are eternal. Can you lighten up? Lighten up on yourself. Lighten up on others. Just lighten up! None of it is really that serious. None of it is really that important. We are not here to save or fix anyone or anything. We just made it up so we would have a good game to play. The funny part is that we forgot we were playing make-believe and became the whole story.

The humor of it all is that we are jesters and jokesters. We love to laugh and create drama. We have reached the moment in time where the Divine Tragedy need be balanced with Divine Comedy. This means we must learn to laugh at ourselves, understanding that we created the whole sordid mess as a play. Earth has been a vast playground where we have been allowed to conjure and create whatever we wanted. We have been in the land of make-believe all along. Of course, the boys would be playing war games, and shooting, and killing. Is that not what little boys do? And all the little girls will be playing dress up and house.

We need to remember that we are not confined to the games we have always played. We need new games. Mostly we need to laugh at ourselves for the silliness we have engaged in, the seriousness, turmoil, chaos, and confusion. It is time to learn how to laugh at ourselves. This is not to diminish the breadth of experience each situation provides, but to give a different perspective so that we unlock ourselves from the cycle of pain and self-inflicted drama.

Look at how creative we are. We are a dream within a dream within a dream within.... You could say we are a drama within a drama within a drama within.... We created the drama that would be the Earth school experience. Then, we came and created drama within experience. Now we are creating reality shows within the reality of life so we can participate in other people's drama. Soon we will be watching a show about housewives watching a reality series about themselves. Wheels within wheels, we do know how to spin the stories. Now, can we just have a little humor around the fact that we do so!

Children have no inhibitions when it comes to joking around, playing dress-up, acting, or making a fool of themselves. They are most content at laughing at themselves. When in their true essence, they are jesters, living and loving life. That is youthfulness. They create the stories and then create new ones. They do not carry the stories into one another or even collect them in bags to carry behind them.

We age because we become too serious and embedded with the density of worry, trapped emotions, and story. Divine Humor has the element of detachment, allowing the stories of our lives but not holding onto them. As each story enters experience, be with it but let it release. In the midst of that, stay light and be the jester, in terms of seeing the many angles and perspectives the story offers. When we are serious, we toss one ball in the air, afraid that it will drop. As the jester in Divine Humor, the story has the perspective to be many balls spinning and dancing in the air. Some will fall, others will not. The jester is enjoying the juggling act, as well as being the one who sees, the one who juggles, and the one who watches. A smile continuously exists in the heart, embracing the experience regardless of whether it is a story of comedy or tragedy.

We are Light. We are Light beings. Our being is to bring Lightness to every experience.

The Essence of Divine Communion

There is no place like home. Home, sweet home. Follow the yellow brick road. Home is where the heart is. I want to go home.

When we begin the jaunt on this planet, we emerge into the world feeling at home. It all may be unique and different, but there is a sense of security that is innate. Some are fortunate to carry that for quite a while. The feeling stems from a deep connection to home. This is not a place or a person. It is the degree to which one feels in union and communion with everything internal and external.

The essence of Divine Communion has no space or separation. Everything is composed within one field. It is all connected energy. When children come in, they are immersed in sensory perception. There is no thought of separation, only discovery and wonder. They are steeped in the body. Intention stems from the heart and gut, the experiential brain matter. Until they are conditioned otherwise, children live from this place of freedom. They know no limitation and are secure in wide-open wonder. They easily dive into the unknown as adventurers.

The field continually reminds us of this adventure. Love shows you yourself in order to know where you are at home. There are many rooms in the mansion, and many mansions in the kingdom. Consciousness can be looked at as rooms within a mansion. Each mansion is a level of created reality. The expanse of all mansions is the kingdom. This is the field and all of it is home.

We can choose where to live in the kingdom. Some choose to live in the rooms of dilapidated mansions, dark and cold. The field does not judge this. It is all home, the full expanse of polarities. In this part of the home, the light is dimmed or distorted, where there are shadows. It is still the field; it is still love. When we are ready to move into another room, or another mansion, it is no different than physically moving. If we take our belongings from one place to another, we bring that old stuff into the new mansion. If we choose to leave the belongings behind, the new mansion has a fresh beginning.

There is only one difference between the way we perceive life and the way children perceive it. We judge where we are by labeling it good or bad, right or wrong, beautiful or ugly. Children are content wherever they are. They are ready to play. The do not judge their surroundings. They accept what is unless they have been conditioned otherwise. They make home wherever they are. Children accept, adjust, and embrace freely. They keep moving forward unless they are taught they receive more attention being stuck.

What we forget, due to conditioning, is that we are everything. The current human is in a quest for oneness. The very quest is an intention of separation. Intention is of the mind, where separation originated. This is the analytical, processing, filing brain. All we really require is acceptance and awareness that everything is the field. Everything is God-stuff. And we are that God-stuff, so it is already one. It need only be treated as such. We do not need to be anointed or blessed into Oneness. We need only make our relationship to everything more intimate and understanding. Intention moves into the heart when we state something from a place of inclusion, not the knowing of exclusion.

Children will play with any child, even if they have just met. They will embrace animals, trees, a puddle of water, even an acorn. They see the beauty. They want to touch it and be with it. They are in relationship with their environment. They are at home in their home. Can you be at home in your home? Can you be at home in the room of the mansion you currently are in? If you move, can you be at home in the new mansion, while still being connected to the other in the field of Love?

This is home. There is only Love. There is only oneness. There is nowhere to go. There is nothing to escape. There is nothing to leave. There is nothing to change. There is everything to embrace. This is Divine Communion. Welcome to your homecoming.

The Essence of Divine Alchemy

11:11 Make a wish. All you have to do is dream. Believe. Create a little magic! Light, Camera, Action! The stuff movies are made of.... Finally, I am losing my mind!

How many have forgotten how to dream? How many have imprisoned their dreams? Have you become too practical? Have your desires been domesticated? Has your imagination been placed on lock down? What excuses take precedence over your life?

Fear can appear in a variety of ways. Its subtle forms are the most detrimental. They cause a slow death, one that turns hope into hopelessness, passion into half-hearted living, and presence into passivity. How evident is that in your life? The weight is directly proportional to the degree you stopped believing—in life, in yourself, in your dreams.

When we are kids, we believed we are invincible. We owned the world and it served us. We lived in the land of many dreams, and our hopes for the future were based on the magic we knew to exist. Some moment came when we bartered those beliefs in exchange for something else.

Life is not only on our side; we are it. We are life happening. Magic flows from our fingertips so easily we do not even realize that we are magicians. As children, we believe—until we don't.

Believing is different than faith. We all have faith, even when we think we have lost it. We either have faith in all that is good, or we have faith in our burdens, ills, and challenges. Believing is either there or it is not. You will either BELIEVE or have fallen victim to beliefs. If you are trapped in belief systems, the magic cannot survive there, because the real you is not there. The real you is the essence.

To BELIEVE is magical, encompassing dreams and imagination. When we believe, we activate miracles in life, because we are in the essence of Divine Alchemy. Divine Alchemy is pure co-creation in, with, as, and through the world. Divine Alchemy is playing in this magical playground with every piece and part of ourselves joining the game. The world plays our game because we BELIEVE to such a degree that only magic can line up. Can you get back to that place of essence?

The essence of Divine Alchemy never leaves us, even in our darkest night. It is the Conversation of the Universe. The magic is happening all of the time. It can't not! We must engage or re-engage with it. There is nothing that is random in life. There are no coincidences or even synchronicities. It is all a divine, cosmic, ongoing conversation. Everything in our world is here as a representation. It is you showing you...YOU! It is also appearing as the magic, the dream, the wisdom. How will you play now? The world is not here to fight with you; it is here to play with you.

Children come in doing this. They talk to trees and see fairies. They dance in the rain and hear the call of the wind. They know the world speaks to them. They are connected and bring in the imagination to expand that conversation. Children are completely in play, and this heightens Divine Alchemy in every moment. You never lost it; it is still here, because you are still here in many shapes, sizes, forms, and expressions.

The Essence of Divine Presence

Hold me. See me. Be with me. Hug me. Love me. Take my hand. See past what I show you. Look into my heart. Know my soul.

Can you look into another's eyes and see who they really are? Can you peer into another's life and feel where they are? Have you opened your heart to another to help them tap into the possibility of who they came to be? Can you create the safe space in the world by being a sacred space yourself?

Within each one of us is a deep well of compassion that is as deep as the Divine. It can never run dry, because our connection to all things is ever present. It, however, can be covered over by the harshness projected by and onto the self. In being covered, it is still the full well, but one that is unable to be accessed.

When in the womb, we are completely protected and cared for. A miracle forms from two becoming the one that we each individualize as. As we birth, we experience care and compassion. But we do not always experience honoring. Much of the world has forgotten how to truly honor one another. How can they if they are not honoring themselves, their humanity, their Divinity? Honor, care, and compassion are essential to the core self.

The small child is extremely empathetic, feeling for even the smallest of creatures with a full heart. It is our natural tendency to care. Innately, we only know love and compassion. What is the factor that most magnifies this ability? I believe it is the state of innocence.

Innocence is untouched and open. It is the precursor for compassion. Children are pure innocence. They seek to discover and know the other. They do this by feeling, not by thinking. They also do this by connecting, not by standing back and watching.

As we have become more and more technologically advanced, we have moved back as watchers rather than engagers. Social media, while creating a form of connection, is literally a "wall" between us as well. Between our education, the walls, and the filters, how can we approach anything from a place of innocence? It is not possible. It is also a way to maintain a level of safety: *"If I do not empathize with you, I do not have to recognize the same within me. If I allow myself to see you from innocence, I risk having to feel the pain for the first time all over again."*

We have gotten away from the true purpose of having life: to feel. Feeling brings the body, mind, and soul into the Presence of all that is Love. This Allness holds the Light and the distortions of the Light. Many of us do not want to see our distortions. But even more so, many do not want to see their *powerful* Light. They had it once before, at birth, but it was too much to shine in this dense world. Many are afraid of their own Light and what that means in terms of their lives, families, relationships, and experience. They prefer being blind in the dark rather than blinded in the truth of the Light.

Being blinded by the Light is significantly different than being blind in the dark. You may say, *"In both cases, I cannot see."* Yes, this is true, because in both cases you are meant to feel. In the dark, you are meant to feel your feelings that desire to come forth. In the Light, you are meant to feel the Presence that you are. When you are willing to truly feel this Presence of guidance, trust, support, and Love in your life, the Light will not shine at you, blinding you; it will shine from within you, Lighting the way for you and the others that will resonate with you.

You are the mighty Presence. Can you be present with that? Whatever your answer, it is always present to you, patient with you, protecting and honoring you.

The Essence of Divine Simplicity

Pebbles. Empty boxes. Sea shells. Bubble wrap. Bouncy balls. Sticks. An ant.

We have overcomplicated our lives, believing we "need" more than we really need. It is not the truth. Once again, we have taken on what is being taught. We are conditioned into having stimuli to take us out of the value of ourselves into the complexity of the world. The fact is, we are not all that complex. Actually, we are very simple in our needs. We are extremely simple when it comes to accessing joy. However, it has become as convoluted as our stories and interwoven belief systems.

If we became really honest with ourselves, we would realize all our stuff is actually making us more miserable, more stressed, and more disconnected. Many would argue that having money, living in a certain neighborhood, or shopping makes life easier and happier; but does it? Are these things simply a band-aid to cover over the true longings?

Think back to when you witnessed a one-, two-, or three-year-old at her birthday party. She tears apart one gift after another, ending up in the corner playing with empty boxes, bows, and bubble wrap. Consider how a child delights in the simplicity of leaves, acorns, or seashells. If you sense deeper, it is not even these objects that has them in her joy, but the connection and experience of togetherness that occurs.

Look deeply within. What is it you most desire? If you look beyond all that is material and go to the heart of what matters, what is all of the striving, hoarding, collecting, and working for? What is it you ultimately want to feel at the end of that? Whatever THAT is, can you create it right now? How may you create it simply?

The needs we have are very basic. They truly consist of time, space, connection, balance, and meaningful creation. In considering the children above, they were in the experience of time and space, having meaningful connection and balance. Nothing else was required; it was all just extra stuff—backdrop. Are you caught up in the backdrop or engaged in the experience?

The essence of Divine Simplicity continually turns us back to what really matters. It is a subtle call from deep within. It is that longing that you feel when everything seems good but something is still missing. Divine Simplicity is the sacred part of you that asks you to let go and trust in the flow by really having what fills you. It occurs with balance, an equal distribution of meaningful work and meaningful play. Divine Simplicity will take you to the point one day where you ask, *"Do I really need all this stuff? Do I really need this identity? Am I striving to achieve a goal that I really could just choose to have right now? Am I taking the long way around to get to a destination that I am already at?"* This recalibration of experience reactivates the essence of Divine Simplicity. In activating greater degrees of simplicity in life, true happiness can surface because you are engaging in more meaningful experiences and connections. In banking the richness of what you now encounter, a new experience of wealth and freedom opens in life. Letting go of the identities associated with accumulation allows for a type of freedom that is unencumbered and open to the discovery of the unknown self. This is what is meant by nonattachment.

The old ways contribute to your enslavement, having you continually become more of who you are, rather than discovering all of who you have not let yourself become. If what you have, in any way, confines you to certain expectations, behaviors, or obligations, you are imprisoned by those things. Can you be the same person if you lost everything? If not, who could you be without them? What pressures and degree of the false self would fall away with those things? I have spoken to many people that have left what they knew their lives to be for something "lesser" and they experience greater freedom and joy. I have seen many who have accumulated great wealth, have a smile on their heart, but have many empty chambers, literally and physically. And there are those who will fall somewhere in between. The question is realizing at each point on the polarity, the scale is weighted between freedom and enslavement, heart and mind, riches and wealth.

Much of this conversation has been about letting go, because we hide behind what we have. Accumulation is relative. A person with very little wealth can be just as attached to his things as a billionaire to his expensive toys. Transcendence is living beyond what exists and knowing what lay beyond that identification. Living simply is a small part of simplicity. Divine Simplicity is grounded in living in the balance. It is the line between have and have not, understanding simplicity is not defined by the direction you go but what you focus on when you get there.

The Essence of Divine Guidance

I can do it! It's my turn. Do it this way! I want it!

This is mine! I can have it if I want to!

Who are you? The son of this one, the daughter of that? Do you come from a generation of medical professionals or one of farmers? Are you Catholic or Hindu or Agnostic? Are you straight, gay, or lesbian? Are you conservative or liberal, Democrat or Republican? Look at the many ways that we separate ourselves. This is just a handful of how we convince ourselves of the lie.

We have been on a quest to discover who we really are, but from defining filters that dilute the ways in which we are able to even recognize it. Our minds are limited by the imprinting taken on from identification. If we only see black and white, how do we ever operate from a perspective of full-blown color? When we know no color, then there is a canvas that can be painted without influence. But if we have no influence, then how would we move? We would move from the essence of Divine Guidance.

If you ask a child where God is, he will point to his heart. If you ask him who is in the trees, or the wind, or a flower, he will say that it is God. Children believe in angels. They believe in themselves. They know they have power. They are confident. Somewhere inside of these little creatures, the essence of Divine Guidance tells them they are kings and queens, sons and daughters of greatness. Something inside of them tells them they have nothing to fear, that there is only Love.

Children do not look at color, race, or religion. They are not interested in which party you belong to or how many moms you have. They want to know if you can love a beetle. They are interested in seeing if you can share. They want to hear if you can honor who they are with time. This way of being comes from the essence of Divine Guidance within them. These sons and daughters of the Divine are given to us as examples of this—until we tell them we know better and teach them who and how we desire them to be.

Moving beyond who you believe yourself to be requires you knowing where you came from, your Divine Inheritance. You are kings and queens of the mighty kingdom. You have been given the gifts and jewels, wearing a crown of Divinity. When you are truly ready to claim this truth by living out your radiance in each moment, the essence of Divine Guidance can flow fully through you. You are no longer wounded; you never have been. You are a Master, the ruler of this reality. It is time to step forward and guide your world from the throne of the wise ONE.

The Essence of Divine Love

I love. I love unconditionally. I love you. I always have. I always will.

We are one. We are the same. We are Divine sparks of Light.

The Divine as me honors, cherishes, and beholds the Divine as you.

Let Love be your Lover. You do not need another. Your need for another was the belief that something was missing, that something outside of you could fill you, bring happiness, and provide life value. When you are in Love, and you are your Beloved, you will feel whole and complete. In that space of completion, you will experience another that is complete and whole, although at that point, it will no longer be necessary. You will be neither alone, nor lonely.

The spiritual misconception is that the Beloved is God outside. You are both, Lover and Beloved. You are God-Being and Human-being. You are both, because God is inside and this recognition is the unification of the self and the SELF. What greater romance could there have been? What more beautiful courtship could exist? This is true union and communion celebrating the Divinity of both aspects of the ONE, celebrating all others as reflections in the playing field of Love.

Have you noticed how children love to look at themselves? They enjoy hearing themselves talk? They cannot get enough pictures taken. One could say there is a touch of narcissism in the early years, as they are so self-absorbed. They truly believe the world was created for them. And they expect everyone else to know the same.

This is not the case at all. They are simply in love with themselves. They are Lover and Beloved combined. They are still not at a point where they have been separated into the idea of Lover and Beloved. They are just in Love. What would you think if you saw an adult looking at themselves in the mirror, the way a child does? Can you imagine being that in love with yourself? Don't you think before creation happened, the Divine Essence had this great Love for itself? To create this vastness and the desire to see itself in multiple ways could only be from ONE who completely utterly loved and celebrated itself. Here is the power we all possess, but we must be willing to recognize that power. Furthermore, we must be willing to completely love ourselves for having it.

There is a fine line between a show-off and pure expression. One who shows off has to talk about it, expressing in ways that needs others to know. This is not full love; it is actually one who seeks love from others, because she has a deficiency for herself. Pure expression just is. It exists for the experience of expressing itself, for itself. It has no need for others to know, but others will.

Does a mountain or stream have to call out? Does a zebra, peacock, or butterfly say, "Look at me"? Does an orchid require your praise to be beautiful? No, because they are all united as the experience of Lover and Beloved.

Love yourself and be-loved by yourself.

The Awakening of the Soul's Magyck: An Activation

Magyck comes from the hot fire.

Embers and ashes, glowing with passionate possibility and resting with the deep knowing of the ability to become, having been and now gone, always beginning and ending at a place which meets others where they are.

It is my personal Divine will and God/Goddess magyckal intention to manifest a life of....

Awareness of what my greatest power is to be placed upon.

Leadership in sacred action.

Clarity for creations serving higher good.

Honor for the Divinity of all individuations, knowing I am not my brother's and sister's keeper, I am my brother and sister.

Exquisiteness that allow me to sparkle, shimmer, and shine!

Mastery of the human experience, mirroring reflections in my outer experience.

Youthful excitement in the YES to adventure!

Play in the Light of Expression

I
want to
play with you.
Wheeeeee!
Higher! Faster! Higher!
Dreaming! Magical! Mysterious!
We are not yet living until fully sensory aliveness.
Beauty shines through the willingness
to breathe dreams and fly.
All angels, all Masters in disguise,
each one may move the energy, transforming,
into wonder and mystery that which is unseen.
Dance in the all-possibility of our discovery.
Transmute...Transform...Transport the mind and heart.
Awaken the power of expression fully and completely.
This wand of creation is given to each one as the inheritance.
Thank the surrogates that raised you. Thank them.
Thank them profusely, whoever they may have been.
Now remember your true Mother...Divine Mother.
Remember your true Father...Divine Father.
and the family of your birthing...Family of Essence.
They have been inviting you to enjoy the game.
Asking you tap into your Magyckal Essence.
Whispering to you of Unique Genius
WE have forgotten to play...
We have forgotten "how" to play.
It is time to remember.
Will you play
with
me
?

Expression is the allowance of the Divine to come through in its full nature. When we hold back expression, we hold back the true meaning and value of our lives and the purpose for which we chose this experience. In not fully expressing, we say to the God of our being that we do not give it permission to be. Expression is celebration of breath, life, spirit, and all that is. We are made in the image and likeness of our creator and that is creation. Creative expression is our Divine birthright. Unique expression is the way we thank all of Divine creation for that right.

Sliding: Wheeeee!

Don't you love a great slide—dry, wet, small, steep, straight, loopedy-looped—just enjoying the ride! There is no hesitance to make the climb, which is always many times longer than the descent. But it is worth it every time. Feeling the air rush past your skin, the sun upon your face, the slickness of the plastic beneath your bum. There are all kinds of ways to express on a slide—feet first, head first, on the back, on the tummy, walking down, walking up, knees up close—and feel the freedom of being alive!

The slide is our life. We can leap into life however we choose, enjoying a fast ride or one where we extend our legs and brace ourselves slowly all the way down. We think we enjoy the way down, but I think we actually enjoy the climb up. Within the climb is the excitement and expectation. During that time, the imagination goes into overdrive coming up with ways that we desire to slide differently. We put so much emphasis on the rapid free fall when what really matters to us is the climb that got us to the top. We do not climb up to go down. We slide down so we can climb back up and see life from the top!

- How many times in your life have you taken the downslide so you could experience the climb again?

- What is it you love about the climb?

- What parts of you are the true expressions of your gifts as you take each step?

- How do you slide through life—head first, feet first, inching your way down, on the fast track, eyes closed, eyes open, hands gripping the edges or hands in the air?

Swinging: Higher! Faster! Higher!

There is no greater feeling of childhood remembrance than being on a swing. The gentle sway of back and forth and the ability to go back and forth, fast or slow, feels freeing. The best part is, regardless if another is helping, we are involved in the ascent. We affect the speed. We swing between control and letting go. There is a balance that exists in the flowing motion of a swing. There is a constant giving and receiving. In those moments, we trust that we are held and allow the movement of going back and leaping forward, always in motion.

Life is like constantly swinging, except we have forgotten we are held. We have forgotten the Divine is behind us, guiding and pushing us as fast, high, or slow as we choose to go. Instead of seeing this ability to move through all of time, we get hooked on what is behind us and stay there, knowing it as only one part of the motion. Or we desire to keep going higher in front, that we do not give credence to the past, which was the balance in getting us so high. It is important to allow the swinging of past and future to be a part of the motion—small parts of it—because what is real is the mighty present and our part in that ongoing motion.

Bubble-Mania: Dreaming! Mystical! Watch them float!

Don't you love bubbles? Blow some! They are magical balls of possibility. They are dream spheres. Every time I blow bubbles, I am mesmerized at the rainbow colors I see. It must mean there is a pot of gold inside—not one we must find, but one we must place inside: a Divine wish, one that floats out as an intention, an asking of the Divine Mother and Divine Father, who never refuse the Divine Child. When the bubble bursts, imagine the desires being released into the ethers to begin the process of becoming real—if we keep believing. We are the pots of gold. We are the rainbows. In fact we are the bubbles of possibility.

Go out with a giant bubble wand and create massive amounts of bubbles. You are entitled to dream and have all possibility. What will you place as pots of gold within these magical rainbow spheres? What words will you anoint your life with as you call each bubble by name? What are you willing to place into the ethers, fully believing in the magyck of your possibility bursting into reality? What will you believe for yourself now?

I am the one who knows, a Divine ONE.

My wisdom empowers the world.

Living my truth is a beacon of Light for many.

I am the Divine example, the true teacher.

I am the Divine expression of authentic living.

I walk in alignment through right-use and fullness of every word, thought, and feeling.

I am Divine action that ripples outwardly in tender waves.

All that I give returns unto me ten thousand fold in the gentleness of Lover cherishing Beloved.

I am the space of the unknown…waiting to become known.

The truth is out!

THE INTEGRATION

The Essence that you are had decided to experience itself in human form, and hence the world was created. Remembrance begins with the invitation, invocation, and initiation. However, those three levels are still in the realms of consciousness, that which floats above and around energetic and etheric realms. The acknowledgement of multidimensionality and the honor of being gods-on-legs requires integration. Consciousness has to be brought into the body and looped back up into Spirit. This infinity loop keeps the flow of experience in a state of constant expansion. The body grounds it. Awareness creates the space for it. The core empowers it. The heart raises it. Energy magnifies it. Spirit breathes it, inhaling the experience of embodiment and exhaling the inspiration that channels down into the body.

Essence is having a multi-dimensional experience. If we open ourselves to more of our sensory perception, we can as well. It is already there; it need only be accessed. In being conscious of the integration process, we may not only be in the flow, but also align energetic grid systems with the Divine Master Plan, the original Divine blueprint. The time has come; be of the Essence.

Into Form

Awareness—Mutation—Transmutation

Awareness is not just being "in the now"; it is presence with full body, mind, and environmental perception. Your physical form and intimate surroundings have the ability to support you. In moving toward a more expansive experience of dimensionality, you have the conscious ability to alchemically induce mutation and transmutation. Through the embodiment of Light, color, breath, and Love, you can focus creative capacity into form.

You have treated this body nonchalantly, providing it with only the most basic of needs. Give permission to the body to go beyond what the mind knows. Your physicality has an intelligence all its own, but you have not empowered it. Your physical body is a living, breathing Universe unto itself. It is amassed of many cells, each with a soul, each with a living history of the world, each with the capacity to evolve. Mutations have occurred in reflection of your shadow nature, carrying that very consciousness. This means, where the shadow inhabited cells or organs, distortion and, at times, disease occurred. This was the mutation of that cell or organ as the soul was imprinted by the higher power: you.

Know you have the power to alchemically change your body. You also have the power to transmute any of the shadowed mutations of cells or organs back into the essence of pure Light. Conscious imprinting of the cells creates positive changes and results in transmutation; magic you may wield if you believe it is possible.

The cells, organs, and tissues of your body have their own function, but they also hold a level of consciousness. In this moment, they are imprinted with the level of consciousness you placed or consistently wear. Some are lesser than others, if you condemned or degraded parts of your body through negative self-talk and self-criticism. Others may have a more heightened consciousness, as areas where you have held pride or celebration. Body image issues are another form of distortion because you are a body of Light, and you are casting a shadow upon yourself. Any and all of this is transmutable. You need nothing outside of yourself. You have the power; you need only have the presence.

You hold the ability to direct and focus attention and Light within the body. In combination with the breath and color, consistent present-moment awareness will support positive evolution. The awareness must hold the essence of Love in the highest frequency you can embody. This is not wishful thinking or intention. This is soul surgery. We each have within us the ability to heal, but we have neither been aware, focused, nor present to the souls that are calling. Awareness also encompasses utilizing the senses in greater capacity, beyond what you have been accustomed to. Your multi-dimensionality is only available to you if accessed and used.

Focus on the body, specific areas at a time. Send deep waves of compassionate love. Bathe these areas by visualizing color, as you move through the spectrum of the rainbow. You are Light, sound, and color. Imprint each cell and organ with the impressions of consciousness you desire to hold. Smile. Hold joy in and around the cells. See them spark with Light, transmuting and glowing as full and vibrant worlds within worlds. Smile. Breathe, imagining this magnificent Universe city light up in ecstatic movement. Smile. Breathe. Give focus to this vast Universe and see how it evolves.

Your environment encompasses your external physical body. It is the many spaces you repeatedly visit. You leave an imprint of your energy when you frequent particular places. In visiting those places, your body is impacted by the many "yous" that have previously visited. You are amplifying whatever has been held previously, if not transmuting it.

This is why certain places have a comfortable feeling and others have an uncomfortable one. Just as you bathe your physical body, your environmental bodies need to be cleansed and given fragrance and care. As in the visualization above, place your attention on these places, blessing them with Love, Light, and power. Transmute what is discordant with your true being.

Build your environments as energetic sacred sites within and around you. This includes the most frequented places of your life: your car, home, work space, general travel route, frequent shopping places, restaurants, and so on. You know where you go consistently, both mentally and physically. It is up to you to match up and align the consciousness and energetic frequencies of your worlds. The higher frequency you are able to maintain, the less other environments or individual fields can impact you.

Into Conscious Awareness

Unknowing—Formation—Transformation

We do not know what we don't know, but also we do not know what we know. The fact is we know too little about too much. This knowledge we possess with such pride is the very thing that keeps us confined. With all that has been learned and acquired, a walk into unknowing is the next step.

Who could you be if you did not know what you know? How might you behave, act, and interact differently in the world? What might you be open to that you would not have been previously?

This is why it is necessary to unlearn. When Adam bit into the apple of the tree of knowledge, all things changed. He actually bit into an apple; he did not take in the tree, nor the world surrounding it. He only took in the apple and that is why his knowledge is limited. He traverses a Universe grander than the knowledge limited by the apple. He became too smart for his own good, and chose to walk in control and arrogance, rather than surrender and trust. The time has come to return what was taken and begin again.

By unknowing who you are, you begin to see the formation that you have become. This knowledgeable self you have evolved into is whom you live breathe and walk. This formation, although you thought it was your truth, has only been a very small version of your full capacity. It has been based completely on what you know. This is less than 5 percent of what IS. Imagine if you tapped into that 95 percent you have not known. Can you consider the possibilities that are available to you and your world?

In dismantling what has been created as your persona, many masks and illusions will start to fall away until you reach the simplest form you can identify with. This could feel like nothingness, the place of "Who am I?" This phase must occur before you may walk the true High Way of transformation, where you venture beyond formation. You now journey into the land of unknown, where all discovery and capacity is possible. Instead of "Who am I?" the question becomes "Who will I allow myself to be?" knowing there is no end to expression. The unique distinction between before and after is the level of conscious awareness.

Into the Core

The Dance—Vision—Voice—Virtue

Transmutation and transformation take you beyond the effects of your distortion. The form you believed yourself to be rests in the upper realms and the head. Expansion of consciousness can only be sustained if brought into the core. It is essential to stay grounded as the walk of the unknown takes place. The heart will lead you into the passionate, wild nature of creation. Embodiment minimizes behaviors of unconsciousness or escape. By bringing consciousness into the body, you bring your dreams into earth. You energize the motion of particles to manifest by being present to the particles as they transmute. Embodiment catalyzes the process, while maximizing the potential of its outer reflection.

The first stage of embodiment is the dance of consciousness within the body. It is the excitement that makes the body move. This dance is both literal and figurative. Will you allow yourself to feel into the excitement? Can you let the body do what it desires as an expression of that joy? We are meant to dance and to move. Your physical expression of this moves the energy and sends it out in waves, empowering the field around you with this ecstatic movement. In doing so, you create attraction and the necessary doors open. Just as the imagination can move into the many realms of possibility, let the body do so by physically and energetically moving many realms.

The second stage of embodiment is vision. This is having sight of what you can see, while holding space for what you cannot. Ground the vision: speak it, write it, and anchor it. Through inner vision, or visualization, place the dream in each part of the body. Let it grow roots from the feet. Have the vision nestled into the legs where trust can be held. Place it in the womb space so that it may gestate. Breathe it into the core so it rests within the fire of creation. Steep it in the heart so that it soaks in love.

The next powerful leap occurs when you are able to share this vision with others. Do this when you feel centered within the vision, having run it through the first four body centers. Speak it from the throat, so it is out in the world. See it at the forefront of your forehead, so you maintain focus. All the while, allow the ever-present waterfall of Light to pour down into the crown so that it floods the body and the vision with the powerful Light of the Essence. This is the rainbow highway of the body. Be certain to travel the rainbow road often.

The final step of embodiment has to do with virtue-all perception. To create the highest frequency manifestation possible, everything must be held in the alignment of truth. This is a simple equation to adhere to for organic creation of the highest order.

Maintain the highest thoughts and conscious living, always going within when discordance arises. Be certain that all language matches the frequency of what you desire to create. Be cognizant whether words used are grounded in love and possibility, or fear and lack. Go within when distortion arises. Cleaning and clearing is a constant process of listening.

Stay in the YES. All action should be in the direction of thoughts and words that are aligned with the truth of the heart. Finally, be true to your vision, and allow your vision to exhibit the truth of you. This is your vision; only you can really see it. You are unique, and your dream will be as well. Although others will appear in support of your vision, understand it needs the guidance of its original Divine parent. While being supported by the village, this

Divine Child will always reflect the lineage from which it came. In living authentically, you will be known by the expressions you bring forth. You never have to scream and shout your truth. It need not even be spoken in a whisper. Your truth will be self-evident; it will be lived and embodied. That will be its loudspeaker. When something speaks evidently, it cannot be ignored, denied, or go unheard.

Into the Heart

Soul Song—Resonance—Symphony

The heart has a calling, and it is answered by the soul singing its song. Just as you have a Divine blueprint encoded with our own unique genius, you carry a tone and a frequency. When you are in the full embrace of your individual truth, your entire energy field sends your song out into the Universe. You are lit up, and your illumination inspires and sparks others into theirs. Living from your heart space in this manner makes you a catalyst for others to not only see their own Light, but to also have the courage to step fully into it.

The embrace of your soul song moves others into your field who are of a similar resonance. We are a self-organizing system. Beyond the principle of like-attracts-like is a field of resonance where individuals with similar dreams, visions, or ideas begin appearing. This is the call of the Universe through many hearts for something to be brought into the field. It is a net that is cast by the song to draw in those with similar melodies because they will harmonize.

In the past, an inspiration would drop into the minds of many people but few would act on it. In this New Dawn, more individuals will be in the YES, desiring to live more authentic lives and acting on their inspiration. More than ever before, many will be willing to bring out their magic, resulting in more and more people bringing forth their soul songs. This step of love, courage, and commitment will create a new field of resonance, bringing these souls together in creation.

The Universe is composed of Light, sound, and color. There is a Divine desire to have a collaboration of souls resound throughout the Universe. As individuations come together in resonance and discover methods of playing together where each person's gifts are honored and celebrated, a grand symphony will unfold. This orchestration of the Universe is the Divine Plan that has always been in place.

The heart is where all of this must take place. As we move into more heart-centered living, our fields of energy will merge more and more. The multi-sensory abilities we possess will come into greater awareness. Distortion will also be easier to see. Each person that recognizes, claims, and embodies the highest Light frequency moves us from distortion to translucence and finally into transparency. This is the transition toward multi-dimensionality. Shadows have provided depth. Translucency has been the cleaning and clearing process, the transition phase between darkness and Light. Transparency is the ability to stand within one's own Light. Ironically, your ability to be transparent is for you more than any other. There is only one here, and it is you. In time, you will discover the full meaning of multi-dimensionality.

Into the Energy

Reflection—Synthesis—Synarchy

We evolve and create impressions upon the world. The outer world is a reflection of the energy that is held. We can gauge who and how we are in this manner. The deeper we embody our dreams and creations, the more strongly it permeates the energy surrounding us. In doing so, we create a world of reflections that support our crawling, walking, and running in the world.

The natural order of the Universe synthesizes many pieces and parts around you, bringing together various necessary components that work together for a greater good. In combining separate elements, a whole is formed. This more complex whole will continue to evolve, bringing together others that have different points of completion. This is and has been the journey to wholeness that so many have spoken of in the past. It is changing, however.

The past brought people with varying strengths and weaknesses together. The New Dawn sees no weakness. Every being is a strong part of the whole, bringing their identifiable genius to complete the abstract artfulness of universal creation. These people recognize each other, coming together as a family who knows they are to play together.

A new emergence is raising groups of people in synthesis. It is movement from wholeness to holiness. From the larger group, a smaller resonant group will begin to form. This fractal family feels an inherent Oneness. They are aligned in mission, vision, and heart. Their genetic blueprints have an underlying system linking them together as they birth something entirely new. This collaboration and co-creation in Oneness creates one-body movement for the synarchy. It will not appear to have a system or structure but will be fully guided. Many fractals will begin from individuals embarking on rebel paths. This courageous leap will activate underlying grid systems, bringing forward others from their specific fractal family. These individuals know one another as Masters and honor each other in that way.

Into Spirit

Intuition—Channel—God-being

Intoxication—Liberation—Immortality

The beauty of life is the experience of infinity as a never ending loop of expanding experience, which is also the continuous rise into Spirit. We are endless and attaining that awareness, moment to moment. As trust increases, and the courage to stand in that truth builds, a completely different awakening takes place. This is the doorway many are upon.

Many have been discovering and developing intuition. It is being given more value in day-to-day life. As more individuals awaken to the Conversations with the Universe, recognition of signs, symbols, and ongoing language will strengthen intuition. Once past the novelty of it, individuals will begin to realize they are continuous channels of information and creation. We are in the Divine field of Love. We are "in Love, of Love, and with Love" always. Staying in a relaxed body and engaging in the lightness and laughter of life further opens the channel for more to flow through. When in the fluidity of life, one cannot deny they are God-being.

There is immense power that comes with acknowledging oneself as God-being, and it requires deep humility. In this recognition, the individual is no longer. In knowing all as God-being, all of life is approached in selflessness, unconditional Love, and acceptance. There is no want, because the being recognizes everything as them and for them. They are able to look past the circumstances of life and into the tapestry that is woven together. In complete humility, everything is enjoyed as experience, so there are no agendas, no needs, and no place to stay or go. This individual is always present to the experience of the moment, and that is God-being.

In fully surrendering identity and living as the constant unfolding experience, with no attachment and no need to control or measure, the new human opens to a level of truth that is both intoxicating and liberating. The sense of freedom from completely letting go of identification is the greatest power of all. When engaging in this form of living, there is no going back to any sort of limitation. Those that come across you will be completely awed and inspired at the level of freedom that is exuded.

You will truly view the world as a playground. This enlightened one might be viewed as the drunken fool but to that soul, all others are the ones under the influence and having had lost their minds. These people can see the great cosmic joke. Inside the "humor-Ahs" nature of the Universe lay the immortality of us all.

The Awakening of the Adventure: An Activation

The adventure stirs from within...

Excited but calm...passionate but clear,

Holding an intention to be the experience as the greatest example of aliveness, always beginning and ending at a place which meets others where they are.

It is my WONDER FULL intention to become the adventure by...

Deepening self-love and connection as the mystery to creating more Love.

Realizing the greater risk is staying where I am, not going where I desire to go.

Expecting nothing less than full cooperation and co-creation from the Universe.

Allowing myself to relax, play, and be free.

Making the mundane as important and Divine as the mysterious.

Intuiting, engaging, and experiencing the core of my being as my guide.

Naturally unfolding myself, without the need to control or know the details.

Giving myself the permission to be bold, creative, and uniquely special.

Activating my gifts and talents, both known and unknown.

Walking in devotion to my heart.

Allowing myself to fully give and receive.

Keeping my language clean and clear in reverence to the vision of Oneness.

Entering the chambers of the soul in service to the inner Universe.

Play in the Light...of Creativity

I
want to
play with you.
See what I see!
Let's build a castle!
Let's mix it all together!
Through conscious creation...
All things remain in continuous flow.
We are creation in each and every breath.
Simply more Divine aspects given opportunity to know.
This unseen sparks through for ways to experience and express.
Part of a grand design of how the Universe grows.
In the Light of co-creation, our own Divinity we will see.
Expansion of minds and hearts are beautifully revealed.
We are many sparks individuated and unique
And we are ONE great galaxy of brilliance
Ever-expanding in rhythm and harmony.
Engage creativity in positive Light.
Our essence is creation...
We will create...even if in a dark night.
Conscious creation is the key
To transcending illusion for reality.
Unbounded ecstasy will be the gift
Of living adventurously.
WE have forgotten to play...
We have forgotten "how" to play.
It is time to remember.
Will you play
with
me
?

Creation is who we are. We are made in the image and likeness of our creation and that is Divine creation. We possess that Divine stuff! Creativity is how the Divine expresses in, as, and through us in each moment. Creation is the one true purpose that removes all ills. Through continuous creation, all things flow. In the Light of co-creation, our own Divinity we get to know.

Cloud Gazing: See what I see!

Do you see what I see? It's a dog. I see a face. It is a man with a fishing rod. It is a dove.

Is it our imagination or our creation? Both. We have both the ability to create and the ability to see what others cannot. It is what makes each one of us special and unique. Just as we see images in the clouds, we also see ideas, solutions, and miracles. As children, we take in everything, from the leaves on the ground to the clouds in the sky. It is all for our wonderment, curiosity, and play. We allow any and everything to not only inspire us but be a canvas for conversation, imagination, and creation. Who could we be if we let ourselves see life as clouds in the sky, bringing us shapes and symbols, meaning and messages, inspiration and ideas.

- How often in your life do you let yourself look up instead of down?
- In what way do you see things that people are unable to?
- How can your ability to inspire and be inspired change paradigms?
- What have the clouds been trying to say to you?

Building Blocks: Let's build a castle!

We are naturally builders. Something inside of us wants to see how high we can build a castle. We keep going with the Legos until the structure falls down, and then we build again. We do this because we know inherently we lose nothing. We also are clear that we have everything within us to rebuild no matter what happens. This is the truth of the human spirit.

Things will rise and fall in life. This is a place of change. We will build and equally take apart life through experiences because we are here to learn, grow, and evolve. We also like creating, and whether we admit it or not, we enjoy a certain degree of drama to keep it interesting. The new human enjoys building and knows that anything is possible!

- What needs to come down in your life?
- What, in your life, do you keep building and taking down?
- What do you naturally build without effort?
- What would you like to build now?

Finger Painting: Let's mix it all together!

Life is a canvas to be filled with color. We have been taught to stay in the lines, to make it neat. Because of this, most paint pictures of what they already know and in the structure that will fit the majority's liking. Instead of finger pointing, let's engage in some finger painting!

The time has come to mix it up, to color outside of the lines. Color off the canvas. Color the entire world. Mix it up, all of the ingredients. Find your own medium. Be your own masterpiece. We are all artists using God stuff to create magic...movie magic!

You have painted your life from the beginning; you have used a couple of dark shades. Lighten up! Add some color. Add some Light to that shadow. Make it spirited, make it surreal, make it soft, make it bright, and make it your self-portrait. It's all you anyway. There is only one of us here...and it's YOU!

- What areas of your life could be more colorful?
- How do you need to lighten up?
- What would you desire your self portrait life master-piece to look like?
- How far outside the lines are you willing to go?

I am Creation.
What shall I imagine?
What shall I create?
What miracles may come?
The miracle that I am creates a world that isn't.
The miracle that I am empowers and energizes the field.
The miracle that I am heals, solves, and reveals.
The truth is I am the Universe.
A Divine ONE.
The truth is I am creating Divine Play.
The truth is I am Love, Loving, and Lovable.
The truth is out!

THE INSPIRATION

We have had it a little backward. We have been seeking inspiration from others. We have wanted clergy, teachers, movies, and books to pull us out of our doldrums. We take some in and become inspired, but slip back into the mundane, seeking out more inspiration and happiness. We paste sticky notes with affirmations everywhere. We use images to remind us of who we think we are supposed to be. We hang onto quotes, crystals, or a pendant to help us remember to be joyful. Those appeared as the message of who you already are!

What are you waiting for to wake up truly inspired and happy every single day of your life? A cure, a lottery win, a lover, a job, a family...a purpose? These lists, regardless of material or spiritual in form, could become never ending. Honestly, neither have anything to do with happiness. These are all external focus and gratification. They focus on an end result as the means to get there. We are using both the material aspects of spirituality and that of the world in the same way: as a crutch. But these crutches do not help us run to the finish line; they merely hold us up where we stand.

I am not telling you to stop using any of the above; I just want you to get beyond your crutch so you realize you can stand on your own. You can run to the finish if you desire. Inspiration and happiness are based on the courage and commitment to freedom and expression in one's own life. Instead of operating from "What do I need to get me there?" move into "What unknown of myself am I being asked to discover?" The happiness is already there. The abundance is as well. Everything you desire is already within you as an experience you have yet to discover. There is a "known" part of you and an "unknown." What you feel is missing in your life is simply your unknown.

We come into the Earth school experience to discover ourselves. However, if we become too focused on what we are discovering about others or believing that external things will create everlasting peace, we have sidestepped the curriculum. Those moving into the New Dawn recognize that they are the inspiration, they are the one to inspire, and they are inspired through the experience of that unknown self.

The byproduct is that others see it, feel it, and are also inspired. However, they will not be able to hold onto it, because it is not theirs. If they act from the inspiration to spark their own experience, they will integrate the energy and become their own source of inspiration. What you see and feel from another is what you have within yourself for awakening. In doing so, you can have everlasting inspiration and happiness flowing through.

To be inspired means to be breathed or to take in breath. This means we inhale what surrounds us. We need only breathe it in if we have forgotten how to hold our own. In yoga, there are three parts to the breath. The inhale, or inspiration, takes in what is outside. Here we fill, by receiving. The expiration, or exhale, takes what is inside and expresses it to the outside. In this case, we empty by giving, allowing an empty vessel for new creation. If this is the case, if we are breathing, then we are life, not just a piece of it.

The segment of breathing that is often devalued or considered wrong is holding the breath. Holding of the breath is the most important part. It is the void, the point of choice. Holding the breath is the choice between living or dying. It is the right to keep or let go. It brings the point of being conscious and unconscious to reconciliation. It is the strategic middle ground between the inhale and the exhale, the center point of infinity.

As you move through challenging places, often times the breath is held unconsciously. This is a level of mind that says, "I have no right to be here. I do not deserve to receive." If you arrest your movement and succumb to what arises, you meet a moment of death: death of a dream, an idea, hope, or the spirit. However, if you were to stay in this place and feel the discomfort of not breathing, you would move beyond it, tapping into the unknown. This is the point of rebirth in each breath. You are at birthing anew in each breath; now be aware of it. Rather than a person counting their breaths toward the end of life, see yourself as a being embarking on new life with every breath.

As you move into knowing yourself as creation, holding the breath can become a conscious choice. Living consciously states, "I have the right to take in and hold life. I have the ability to take in and hold Light. I may honor what I have inspired and express its fullness as new life and creation." Live who you truly desire to be. In doing so, every day will be an inspired and happy one.

Do I breathe you? Or is it that you breathe me? As I sense my breath, I feel the gentle push of air from the outside in, as if you bring me to life in each moment. As I exhale, I feel the sweetness of being full that I long to empty and feel you again.

Hold me tenderly as I am guided into the unknown. Place a Divine salve on the places of my heart that have hurt deeply, one that eases the pain and allows me to dive farther into it that I may know its beauty. In the moments I try to make sense of life, help me lay down that burdensome frustration for the peaceful wonder of creation. Sprinkle the embers of love upon me as I view tragedy, so I lay in the sacred valley of the heart instead of the many stories the mind would twist and turn. Let forgiveness and compassion stand in the face of all fear...tearing down the walls of my many lives, and of many unclaimed masters.

Provide me understanding that there is a larger picture I cannot see, that I need not know because I am an eternal being of Light—always whole, healthy, and alive.

I am a little child upon the lap of life, reclaiming my lost innocence, because I can; embracing my beauty, because I am; inhaling the exquisiteness of my being, because it is; breathing in the entire landscape of Oneness as the playground before me. Shall we play? I long to play—free and fluid, unstructured and flowing, excited and alive!

Breathe me. Breathe into me the life I thought was lost, but need only be lived. Breathe into me the miracle that I have always been. As I am inspired with the breath of Grace, I am possibility waiting to happen. I truly am the ONE I have been waiting for. I am the ONE to celebrate and be celebrated.

What I hold in breath, I am free to release. I am allowed to make space for something new. I am the blessing when I share who I am. I exhale inspiration through right word, right thought, and right action, as I learn, grow, rise, and experience. In grace full alignment, I calibrate and release right creation, continuing the lineage of my origin, Mighty Presence.

In Spirit I awaken, knowing it takes a village to raise the child; within me is a grand Universe. In deepening the connection to All that is, I move higher and higher. I merge the Universe within with the world surrounding me, creating connection and Oneness. In my being, I know every son and daughter is everyone else's son and daughter. I empower love, peace, and blessings upon humanity, as I love, bless, and embody harmony within. I recognize my power and my presence. I recognize your power and your presence. I recognize the Mighty Presence of All things. Yes, please, and thank you.

My name, Simran, has a sacred meaning. It is considered a sacred practice involving sound, repetition, and color. Simran signifies one close enough to whisper into the ear of God and have wishes realized. It is the repetition of God's name with utter reverence and the deepest love of the Lover. We are each that. We are all given that grace; each desire is that granted gift. Every inhale drinks in more of the Divine Essence; every exhale is God-being grace fully experienced and expressed. This is the breath; you are simran.... From the lips of the Divine to the ears of the Divine. From your Divine lips to your Divine ears. After all, there is only ONE here. You are the ONE speaking. You are the ONE listening.

The Breath of Innocence

You are the Divine Essence, the ONE who knows and the UNKNOWN. The grace that is to be bestowed is GRACE upon yourself. This is not something to be handed down or extended from some other more powerful. You are THAT. You have the power to bestow your own. The first inspiration of Grace is Innocence, where you may see yourself in the full wonderment of all that you are. Innocence is pure openness, availability to what is in front of you.

We are children at play, here to explore and build. Our imaginations are endless fields to cross, and this planet is the realm in which we may see those ideas unfold as physicality. To be limited is likened to capping a waterfall, but that is what has been done. The rules and regulations, laws and decrees, structures and systems, the walls and fences, the grades and measures, the plans and projects...they exist as a means of control. Controlling what?

One cannot control a wave, nor the ocean behind that wave. One cannot control lava that flows, nor the volcano when it erupts. One cannot keep the rain from falling when the sky opens. Why stop the breath of innocence from living its full life? We are children by design who decided to grow up. Our best thinking got us here. It's time to feel our way out.

What if we were to return to innocence, children completely at play? What if there were no structures? What if we had no systems to tell us what to do, nor laws to tell us how? Would we crumble? Would we fall? Would we crash or devolve? Is that not what we are doing anyway?

What is behind the creation of structure, rules, government, and systems? Could it be fear? Could it be the loss of innocence that has guided these things into formation? If so, are they grounded in distortion, the shadow of the light?

Can we be innocent once again? And if so, can we allow there to be a world at play—no systems, no rules, no laws? Could we discover how to get along? Would we play well together?

Perhaps the imagination could soar. We may self-organize. Creation would magnify, spontaneously occurring between many. Innocence may open a new way. Through exploration and individuality, hearts and minds would have wings with which to fly. The imagination could run wild and, as nature, we would begin to self organize. As with the Universe, Divinity and infinity would line up. Instead of being a part of life, the breath of innocence would open the world to aliveness.

A return to innocence is calling from within. The child forgotten, orphaned eons ago, has worked too hard and too long. This Divine Child is ready to play. I release all things. I let go of all constructs. I begin each day with renewed innocence. I allow my imagination to soar. I release all inhibitions. I romp through this vast playground that has been presented before me. Do not tell me of the impossible, because I am a child who knows without a doubt that I'm possible!

The Breath of Beauty

Tell me what makes your heart break. What makes it full again? Tell me how you shut down and when you became lost. What brings you back to life? At what moment were you found? What does it look like when you have disconnected from your spirit? Speak of the magic when your spirit soars. Show me the face of your immense pain. Let me see the Light that sparkles when you are in joy.

This is the breath of beauty. It has two parts. The Allness of beauty holds space for every experience and every emotion. It is the inhale in its allowing, in its natural balancing. It is the expanse of every emotion in complete intensity. Can you embrace the beauty of life in this way? Can you hold all of that beauty as you? The grace of this breath provides possibility in every experience that arises. You are granted the full radiance of each emotion. Do you accept these encounters? In doing so, you become the experience, the witness, and the expression of each emotion. What is more beautiful than that?

The other side of beauty pertains to the space of emptiness. This is what remains after the exhale. It is the void where nothing exists. Have you ever found yourself speechless, where no words could be spoken? Have you ever experienced a state of amazement, where no thought passed through your mind? Imagine something exponentially greater than this. What if there exists a place of such emptiness that it holds true beauty, beyond which you have ever known?

If you glance upon the many faces around the world, you may not think there could be anything more beautiful. And then, what about snow capped mountains, glistening streams, and fields of wildflowers? How could those be surpassed? But this beauty never ends: rainforests and rainbows, exotic fish and fabulous feathers, a full moon and starry skies, the brilliant golden sun. And this is all you—yes, you. If this degree of beauty exists in time and space, imagine what lies beyond what we know. Beauty in the emptiness is timeless and boundless. It lives in the imagination that has not been explored. It resides in the areas of the heart that have yet to be opened. Breathe...just breathe. Inhale and exhale. Have reverence for the beauty that you have and you hold from this day forward, for better or for worse, in life and in death, till you unite all parts.

The Breath of Exquisiteness

Divine Essence that I am, let me be my self and let me BE the SELF. Steeped within me is the Divine giggle, an ecstatic "AHA Ha Ha," the creative chortle and a most graceful guffaw at the magnificence of this Universe. How exquisite that we are such unique, radiant individuations, yet all ONE being. This is the ultimate Divine practical joke. We are not here to get comfortable in our being, because we are change happening. We are not here to be imitation. We are each a Rebel walking. Individually, we strike our own paths, forge new ways, and Light up the world. And in doing so, we create the pieces and parts of the greatest puzzle of all, one whose face will not be known until each finds their exquisite place.

The Rebel is the epitome of exquisiteness, because there is an adventurous energy at play. It is an inspired desire from within to create change within one's own life. There is no desire to follow another, nor is there desire to have followers. The One steeped in their exquisiteness just wants to play and bring out the brightness that lay dormant in the world. The Rebel is here to live full-out, willing to laugh at themselves and life, from the state of innocence and beauty. In their individuation, they seek to experience massive creation amongst those who can play the game with them. They are not here to accomplish anything, because they understood the riddle. There is nothing to accomplish. They are not here to fix or save, because there is nothing that demands that level of seriousness. Nothing in life requires a dress rehearsal, because this is a live performance.

The inhale breathes everything in playful Oneness. The breath, when paused and held in the body, is the knowing that all is illusion. The breath held is the full experience of what is real, as attention moves continually inward while the outside fades from awareness. When this breath can be held no longer, an exhale slowly seeps outward. The exquisite One relishes immersion into the emptiness, into the fullness, and especially the unknown.

When a person breathes in the exquisiteness that they are, nothing holds them back. There is no experience that can be called an obstacle or challenge; it is all creative play. It is part of the ongoing adventure. Exquisiteness embodies passion, sensuality, sexuality, silliness, wildness, and freedom.

When you breathe in your own exquisiteness, you live for no one other than yourself. This means you stand in the complete transparency and vulnerability of who you are and what you stand for, and are available to what is infinitely possible. You not only believe in infinite possibility, but are also anchored in all-possibility. There is a deep and inherent trust in and of life, because you realize the Oneness of life, its dance with creation.

The Breath of Oneness

I long to be in the world, but not of it. Oh yes, I forgot—I am. Let me embrace that. If that be the case, then Oneness would be the transcendence of all that keeps me individual and separate. Transcendence would not mean that I ascend, leave, or separate from. In transcendence, I dive more fully into life, stay the course with full presence, and connect the dots of all that I am.

For me to be ONE with all that is, I let go of my judgments, perceptions, and perspectives. I release naming, definitions, and identifications. I see that all is Divinely orchestrated. I accept that only one thing is truly happening, and it is good.

In the breath of Oneness, I inhale my surroundings as individuations of myself. Everything that appears in my awareness is an aspect of me, illustrating me. Oneness is the world speaking to me, about me, as me, for me to know myself. There is only One and it is me, and it is good. The moment has come to fully receive all that I am.

In the intersection between inhale and exhale, where the breath is kept in and the body is full, I experience detachment that frees the world from any prior cords I have held in place to distort my wholeness. I experience detachment that allows the allness of me to calibrate to its highest resonance. I detach in a way that honors the holiness that I am in all expressions.

As I exhale Oneness, it is the well of deep and unconditional Love that is the core of my being. This universal Love is the illumination that has been inside all along, that I have kept myself from seeing. The exhale is the Mastery of this mystery. In that expression, I recognize my self, and all other aspects of my self, as the field that has been Oneness all along. What I did not know was that I dreamed a dream where I dreamed that I was dreaming. And this continued for a long time.

In my slumber, I created a magnificent story of falling from grace. I created man and I created woman, in an attempt to unify and create a Divine Child. But within the dream, I fell asleep. The stories layered upon one another as generations of history and her-story kept unfolding. In wormholes and tunnels, through space and time, I have travelled to reach this moment where I may unite all the fragmentations of my self.

In this moment, I may reconcile all generations, cultures, religions, and storylines of the great novel I became caught up in. Now, I bring together those pieces and parts. I hold the key of forgiveness for creating an unsafe and unjust world that holds fear and darkness. It was my own grand design, one as sacred and holy as I am. I come from Divinity; I can only be Divine. What I create would have to be divine as well.

What an imagination I have had, albeit it unconscious. What a play I have engaged, in darkness and in Light. I am creative capacity. I align all things in Oneness through conscious play as I transcend dreaming to become the fully awakened dream, breathing deeply in Oneness, as Oneness.

The Awakening of Pleasure: An Activation

Eons of devotion have brought you to this moment. Call forth your due now.

You need only give yourself permission to receive. Awaken dear one and experience pleasure, know every sensation. You are sensation-all!

My being opens fully and completely to knowing all the sensory pleasures life allows as an intention to experience and express...

Devotion to the ever-unfolding creative capacity of everything and everyone.

Intimacy, in the most sacred sense, with all aspects of my unknown nature.

Veneration for life, animate and inanimate.

Insight to how others think, feel, and know.

New ways of looking at old problems and issues to bring about solutions.

Empathetic listening to the parts of myself that are Mother Earth calling out.

Uninhibited action.

Never-ending second-by-second joyful presence, regardless of what appears.

Immeasurable Unconditional Service and Love for all.

Overwhelming gratitude for the gift of this Earth school.

Now...and knowing.

May your dreams be sweet. Your night, the vast space of magical ether, awaits your infinite presence. May your lids sacredly hold the Divine Light to be carried through. May their opening reveal brilliant portals for expressive creation to manifest physically. May the day provide a clear and open landscape for play. May Light reflect down into the body and out into your world with Power, Freedom, and Grace, sprinkled generously with pleasure and Possibility!

Play in the Light...of Unknowing

I
want to
play with you.
I can't see you!
But I can hear you!
The center of my world!
Do not tell me where I am going.
Do not tell me who I am.
Do not show me my vast possibility.
Let me discover it from where I stand.
Play with me, Universe.
Bring me the messages.
Present the gifts in coincidence...
Ahhh...the synchronicity and signs!
Let my discovery of them be mine to align.
In the moments of my walk,
I shall learn how to listen, see, and talk.
It is all a gift resting in the vast unknown.
The multi-dimensional me I am waiting to be shown.
I had forgotten the essence of my nature...
I have forgotten to play...
I forgot "how" to play.
It is time to remember.
I will to play
With you
each
day
!

Show me your vast unknown, the playground of life. Awaken my eyes, dear Father, to the magic of the night. Open my ears, Great Mother, that I hear your every beck and call. Hold me in your loving arms as you have since long ago. Now I am ready to remember the truth that I am. Let me grab your finger as I crawl, walk, and stand. But this time, I shall not forget the innocence of a child. It is from the wonder of those eyes and ears that I will be truly alive.

Marco Polo: I can't see you, but I hear you!

Moving through the water, the eyes are closed. All other senses heighten to catch the subtle messages that one is near. It is sensed through the movement of the water, listening to the sounds of breath, feeling in ways not even conscious of. We know we are not alone. In fact, we know we are many. In that moment, we are the one; in another, we recognize and touch another one. WE are all in the water, all in the game. WE are all sensitive and senseless. We are all tapping into what we cannot see but what we know exists.

Is this not the dance between human and essence? What we have not seen is that the ONE we seek is all around us, in the water with us, playing the game. It is our own illusion that it the ONE rests outside of us, away from us, watching the game. It is all here. Whenever we call out, we get a response. Whenever we stop to listen, we feel, sense, and know ONE is near.

Open your eyes and see how the Divine is all around you as other ONEs. Who can you align with, play with, enjoy the game with?

Simply close your eyes and call out. Then, become still and quiet, and allow your senses to guide you to ONENESS.

Hula-Hoop: The center of my world!

You are the center of your world. You maintain its motion on your own. As you rotate and center in your core, you provide the rhythm necessary to keep your own sphere at whatever level you desire and at whatever speed. You are engaged in a dance, a joyful one. You are immersed in experience—your own. You are one with your surroundings and collaborating in a way that you remain connected, expanding and in the flow. As the dance continues, the circle of influence that surrounds you can be lifted high over head, moving along the arms of giving and receiving, balanced along the trunks of trust and brought back to center at any time, always remaining connected, in play and in motion.

Sounds like great hooping. Yes, could be. Sounds like a great experience of life. Yes, it is.

- Every time you stop, does everything around you drop and stop?
- Are you carrying the ring of the world on your back or are you evenly distributing the weight so that it is balanced?
- Do you move with your world in a rhythmic manner, or are you trying to control the direction and flow?
- Are you opening to a circle of influencing and allowing it to ebb and flow?

I am Love, Divine Love.

I am unconditional pure Love.

I see everything through Love's eyes.

I hear everything in listening through Love.

I feel into everything as Love embracing a small child.

I know everything as Love, mothering and guiding and nurturing.

*I act upon calls for Love with strength and action,
fathering with gentle discipline and wisdom.*

As Love, I see beyond the surface and into the core.

*In Love, I hold the space for all to attain the highest
frequencies of its capacity.*

Of Love everything births, grows, dies, and is reborn.

*With Love, I engage in simran, known as the deep repetition of
Divine sound and light in communion with itself.*

I am Love's sweet whisper, because Love need not do more than that.

In Love, of Love, with Love, as Love...I AM

The truth is out!

THE ILLUMINATION

Light is always present. Illumination exists. Until you awaken to the brightness that shines, it is not lit. If it is not apparent to you, then it cannot be seen by anyone else. What good is Light if it is in a closed room? If your illumination remains on the inside, how will it to Light up the world? You may say, "If there is nothing out there, what need is there to Light up the world?" The world is your reflection. It exists as a means to gauge your inner world. Because you have eyes that see outward, you are unable to see what is inside. The world is your projection screen, always displaying what is within the projector.

Illumination happens when you have not only released the small "i," but also the larger "I." It identifies with no thing. It is pure Light. The Illuminated One has reached the enlightened God state in full knowing, in words, beyond words, and even in the space between the words. Here lies pure truth. The Illumined One just IS.

These Ones of Light are no longer just living; rather, they embody aliveness. They have moved from form to formlessness. They venture beyond space and time, into timelessness. They have released their bounds and boundaries to experience boundlessness. They have transcended all longing into belonging. Illumination is the divinely inspired embrace of itself: Light Being.

In Light of Living Into Aliveness

Will you have this? Will you allow it? Will you move beyond having a life? Will you step past living? Are you ready to experience aliveness?

In this moment I open to my greatest Self, that part of me I have not yet known, cannot fathom, nor comprehend the courage of, or fully understand the expanse of inherent gifts. I acknowledge that I am the whole One and the Holy One.

I open, allow, and receive ME in the fullest, most loving embrace. I am ready to play larger than I ever have. I give myself permission to move beyond living, making a living, or having a life. I seek to know my aliveness, and I shall. And, those in my life, especially the naysayers, will just have to respond as they do.

My grace is the blessing of life. My gratitude is being alive. I now awaken to unfettered aliveness! I avail myself of every experience and expression that tempts me into being alive in wild, bold, passionate, and creative ways. I am in discovery of the powerful writer, singer, actor, artist, humorist, and creator that waits to emerge from within me.

I ask every cell within my being to calibrate to its highest frequency of Light. I request that my Divine blueprint access the energetic matrix that is my illumination. I call forth the alignment of my energetic circuitry, soul templates, sacred geometric forms, and Earth grid systems to support my attention and intention of aliveness. I ask my angels, guardians, guides, spiritual advisors, body deva, and spirit team to illuminate my spiritual human form into the Light of Aliveness.

In Light of All that is, in Light of All that I Am, so be it and it is so.

In Light of Form Into Formlessness

Can you cherish the form? Will you allow the forms to dissolve? Open to the formlessness of your being?

I am freedom. I know form, but I am formless. I honor and bestow gratitude on all forms that have been within my experience as the structures necessary for my awakening. I acknowledge that rules, guidelines, and structures have been put in place as a way to move through fear and avoidance of the unknown. I choose to break free of any and all forms, structures, or methods that I have believed in. I dissolve those that have a hold on me or that I have held onto. I step beyond fear and into the unknown. The unknown is not to be feared, because it is the expanse of my greater Divine Beingness that I have yet to discover.

Form and formlessness happen through me. From these identities, I transcend the illusion called life. Truth lies within, beneath, and beyond the veils I've draped inside as thought, belief, and perception. What lay beyond what I have called ME is real. I embody the physical, as I am increasingly aware metaphysically of the all-encompassing Presence that I am. My great Unknown self awaits my recognition.

I have this body, but I truly have not known it. It is the form that carries me through this physical experience but it is beyond a mere vehicle. It is an extension of this experience that I am, but it is not all that I am. It is a Universe that I am to embody and cherish, to guide and give to, to keep sovereign and at peace. In the more of me I get to know, I realize that form meets form. These communing and expanding forms eventually have no walls. The air, the sky, the Universe—I am all of these things.

In moving beyond walls, I shall find my formless nature. I call forward the consciousness of my physical human form, the nature and presence of all forms in and as my life experience. I call forward my bodies, physical and energetic, and all related blueprints, grids, and plans. I ask every cell within my being to calibrate to its highest frequency of Light. I request that my Divine blueprint access the energetic matrix that awakens the consciousness of formlessness. I call forth the alignment of my soul templates, sacred geometric forms, and universal grid systems to support my present moment awareness of form to formlessness. I ask my angels, guardians, guides, spiritual advisors, body deva, and spirit team to illuminate my human form into the Light of Formlessness. I ask to be taken beyond all forms; let me engage in complete devotion within the formlessness of my being.

In Light of All that is, in Light of All that I Am, so be it and it is so.

In Light of Time Into Timelessness

What time is it? Will you move beyond the limits of time? Are you ready to experience timelessness? Will you step beyond the past and turn back from the future?

I no longer ask, "What can I survive? Achieve? Move beyond?" Those are tests of time. I am not here to be tested. I am here to have the time of my life. Time is necessary only as a precursor to the experience of timelessness. I can stop time. I can make time. I can have time. I can be timeless.

This is my time. I seek an understanding of the ME that is timeless. I am timeless. I am here to save no one. I am not to rescue anyone, nor heal anyone. The very thought keeps both locked in a time of pain. I recognize the whole and Divine nature of others. I honor their power and choice to be, do, and have whatever is their consciousness. Only they may set themselves free. In choosing timeless living, I set myself free.

My dreams and desires require for complete fruition only my time and the timelessness of being in present moment Oneness. As I live in the presence of all creation, I am the living meditation and prayer of all time. Each moment asks my wholehearted and holy-hearted commitment, not my consideration. Anything less than full commitment is a waste of my time.

It is my soulful desire and heartfelt intention to experience myself as timeless ecstasy. I am complete devotion in and to God-being, as the full nature of all creation. I am alive in celebration fully experiencing each moment as moment-US. I encounter the beauty that is beyond words. I open to experience grand mystical encounters, conversations with Masters of the Universe, and a communion with the seen and unseen. I find myself in the timeless spaces and places where all meet as One.

I experience complete unity with all things. Timelessness is the death of all fighting. There is no fight. There is no struggle. There is no need. Timelessness is presence, full immersion with no-mind.

I call forward the keepsakes and keepers of time. I beckon the consciousness of all ages and memory. I call forward my incarnations, my physical human form, and my future ascended Master. I request all blueprints, grids, and paths calibrate to the highest frequency of Light. I call forth the alignment of my soul templates, sacred geometric forms, and Earth grid systems to support my present moment awareness and synchronization of Divine timing. I ask my angels, guardians, guides, spiritual advisors, body deva, and spirit team to illuminate my spiritual human form into the

Light of Timelessness. I bring into congruence all time; let me lay within the timelessness of my being.

In Light of All that is, in Light of All that I Am, so be it and it is so.

In Light of Bound Into Boundlessness

Will you let go of what binds you? Will you be boundless? Will you step past all restrictions, encasements, and ties? Will you be free?

I acknowledge that the boundaries of my life have been self-imposed. I am aware that I believed binding situations to be a necessary part of my evolution. No one kept me bound. I placed the ties, strings, and cords that bound me to people, circumstances, and experiences. I am the one to release these threads of attachment in any moment. In expanding beyond my personality and identity, I move toward boundless living.

I choose to lift all ceilings, remove all walls, discard all foundations, and demolish any infrastructure that limits my movements, dreams, passions, or play. I accept the unlimited potential and infinite possibility that exists within and beyond me as me. I embrace aliveness as boundless love, complete freedom, unlimited grace, and abundance beyond measure. I open to receive this in all ways, shapes, and forms that are in my highest good. I allow the highest capacity of creation to unfold as I selflessly serve in sacred inspired action. I magnetize a synarchy, uniting my fractal family. We engage in celebration, play, light, sound, and color in the most magnificent displays of creative expansion honoring each individuation, but serving the whole.

In Boundlessness, I live life unfiltered and unfettered. I have fun. I am in love, of love, with love, expressing as love. The echo of my divine giggle begins deep and rises high and wide. I am adventure. I am living inspired, while inspiring and being the inspiration. I am in Holy relationship to my creative God Goddess awakened to the courtship of the nebulous, open, and vast unknown.

I call those I have bound and felt bound to. I beckon all limited thinking, glass ceilings, and barriers to be released. I call in the consciousness of supreme, sacred sovereignty. I bring forward my generations, lineages, incarnations, and stories. On behalf of my physical human form and future Ascended Master Self, I request all blueprints, grids, and paths calibrate to the highest frequency Light Being. In complete Oneness and alignment with my soul templates, sacred geometric forms, and Earth grid systems, I empower and free myself to the far reaches of present moment awareness. I ask my angels, guardians, guides, spiritual advisors, body deva, and spirit team to illuminate my spiritual human form into the Light of Boundlessness.

I call forward all hearts that are ready to open and connect. I bring awareness to my entire being in, as, and of the field of Love, encompassing all that I see as Love or the call for Love. I know what I see is me. I have the power to transmute and transform my world in full conscious co-creation. I call in the consciousness of supreme, sacred sovereignty and unconditional Love. I call forward my generations, lineages, incarnations, and stories. On behalf of my physical human form and future Ascended Master Self, I request all blueprints, grids, and paths calibrate to the highest frequency Light Being. In complete Oneness and alignment with my soul templates, sacred geometric forms, and Earth grid systems, I empower and free myself to the far reaches of present moment awareness. I ask my angels, guardians, guides, spiritual advisors, body deva, and spirit team to illuminate my spiritual human form into the Light of Boundlessness.

In Light of All that is, in Light of All that I Am, so be it and it is so.

In Light of Longing Into Belonging

What have I been seeking? Will I choose to long or belong? What would Love do now? In Light of the Lover and the Beloved or Longing and Belonging, who am I now?

I have been seeking you, when all the while I have really been waiting for me. This longing has been deep within my soul. I chose to leave myself. I chose to forget my reality. I chose "ill"usion. I now see the full picture.

My mind has been longing for something to empty it. It has been dreaming of that day it would be silenced. By what? Complete knowing? No, by complete unknowing. It has been thinking of all that could fill it. I could not know full-fill-meant space, timelessness, and boundlessness.

My heart has been longing for someone outside. When would that "one" come that would fill my days and hold me at night? Where is that "one" that would know my every desire and dance in movement with me? Was it to be the one who "sleeps," that being who has carried me into their dreams, sometimes their nightmares? Or has it been the enlightened one who speaks of truth and love and compassion, but may or may not embody it?

Who are all these characters I surround myself with? Do they knock on my heart's door to show me who I am? Perhaps they arrive to show me who I am not? Either way, they let me know of the longing that rests within me. All the while, they are leading me to Belonging. Until now I have swam the currents of longing. I am coming upon the shores of belonging. No man is an island, but ONE is the ocean and the shore.

My soul has been longing for completion. I have been walking toward my ascension. Who knew true ascension lay within the deep dive and depths of the body? Where is it I will be going? How silly that I do not realize that I am already at the top looking around? It is from here that I see the murky depths, while also flying in the clouds. It is from this vantage point I know when I fall, and how I rise and then fly. How could I not see I am already in ascension? What a playground I have been skipping through all along! I have enjoyed each game and tried each activity. I have created my own world with the seriousness of a child at play. My imagination ran away with me.

In my longing, I desired to come home. In my longing, I became tired of the play I created. It became work. It was too hard. It made me too serious. I forgot why I was here. This is why I have been longing. When I moved off into my own world, it was not that all others left me; I left me. I left all others. No one betrayed me; I betrayed me. I believed all of the stories of a distant heaven. In doing so, I created a living hell. This was part of the game I called life. How could I know heaven and hell were one in the same? Both existed in my mind. I left the real playground for the illusory one in my mind—one that feels real and looks real, but is not really. I see the Light. I am the Light. My longing is now in the Light of Belonging.

The ways I have seen do not resonate with me any longer; they do not feel free, flowing, and clean. They are exclusive rather than inclusive, even though the masks try to appear different. "This world is the way it is," so they say. This is a world of longing. I will create a new world of belonging. I will be the Lover of the world. All humanity shall be my Beloved.

I leap boldly into a new play. In this new world, I am the innocent one with an open heart. I do not have to know the details of this live adventure, because it is happening inside of me. I have no need to control it, because I am clear, knowing something larger is at work, fully guiding, protecting, and supporting me. I can dive into the unknown. I am open. I am willing. I am celebrating who I am, whether others can or cannot. My outer world will reflect this beautiful new play as I embody Love, Courage, and Commitment. I trust. I trust completely.

I realize now all those I have been seeking love from, on the outside, have only appeared to show me the love I need recognize, awaken, and behold within myself. Another's love is no longer necessary because I am "in Love" always. I can choose if and when I desire an experience of another, knowing I am really still experiencing myself, my Oneness. It is One reflected as Lover and Beloved, disguised as two. No other Love is required because the Love of ALL is available. I am open to receive the Love of one. I am open to receive the Love of many. I am open and available to Love and being Loved by all.

In my belonging, I create something new and different, founded in Love and connection, based on freedom and courage, steeped in creativity and confidence. I climb the ladder of the soul, unlocking the keys within my DNA, revealing the strands of Divinity that are held in the ethers of grace. I release the jewel that I am. Each cell within me vibrates its soul frequency of Light in full resonance of my belonging. I am a library of consciousness, holding all time and space, memory and future, history and her-story. I am a sacred living text. I attune all codes of longing into the highest sound, color, vibration, and Light of belonging.

As my physical human form and future Ascended Master Self, I Invite, Invoke, Initiate, Integrate, Inspire, Illuminate all blueprints, grids, and paths calibrated to the highest frequency Light Being. In complete Allness and in alignment with my soul templates, sacred geometric forms, and Earth grid systems, I Love and Be-Loved to the far reaches of present moment awareness. I ask my angels, guardians, guides, spiritual advisors, body deva, and spirit team to flood my spiritual human form into the Light of Belonging.

I invite the Rebel in my own life. I invoke the Lover. I initiate the Beloved. I integrate my longings. I inspire and am inspired. I illuminate the Lover and Beloved as ONE.

In Light of All that is, in Light of All that I Am, in Love, of Love, with Love, I AM, so be it and it is so.

The Awakening of Freedom: An Activation

I am free like the wind whispering through the trees. I am free like the waves washing in and out. I am free like the rain showering all with my Love. I am free and Divine, in all places, at all times. I need only remember this and bring my senses in union and communion to this truth, always beginning and ending at a place that meets others where they are.

It is my intention to expand beyond all boundaries—physical, mental, emotional, energetic, spiritual—for the experience of freedom by...

Feeling Excited About Reality, a new acronym for arising F.E.A.R!

Opening my body through various forms of movement!

Raising my hand for new experiences!

Gracious living, being graceful, and knowing grace!

Inspiring, being inspired, and being the inspiration!

Voicing my truth, my love, and my bliss!

Exciting connections open doors of opportunity and magical meetings of collaboration!

No doubts!

Exploring undiscovered talents within myself!

Singing at the top of my lungs, in the shower, in my car, in life, from my Spirit!

Sculpting time, as magical clay, to fit my schedule!

Freedom is not yours to give me. It need not be earned or fought for. It is mine to give to me. In every moment, I have choice. Either I choose an excuse or to see limitation, or I choose to release myself to what I desire. Forgive me, "for I give me" the space to create. For in giving myself my own dreams, desires, and wishes, you will see you too are free to be who you desire to be. I do not know what that looks like, nor do I need to know. I do not need the details or a plan. I need only free myself from this linear thinking, because I am a self-organizing system that organically creates a perfect design. I am the seed that only need be the seed until I am no longer. I am the stalk that has no desire for leaves until they appear. I am the blossom that suddenly appeared but was never longed for, only celebrated in the moment, as is each point of my being.

Play in the Light of Nebulosity

I
will to
play with you.
I can do it!
I can leap as high as I desire!
There are no limits because we are unlimited.
There is no need because we are Source and Supply.
There is no boundary because we are boundless being.
There is no time because we have all the time in the world.
I do no fit my spirituality into my life; my life is my spirituality.
I am the imperfections and the perfection.
Every experience is a moving meditation.
Every expression comes from union.
Every endeavor is communion.
I am the visible and invisible. I am the Light and the dark.
I am the revelation. I am the inhale and the exhale.
I am the praise and the prayer.
I am the celebration...a Divine ONE!
I have not forgotten the essence of my nature...
the presence of joy, play, and spontaneity.
My childlike innocence and wonderment is essential...
I never lost my Divine connection or the meaning
of being a child of the Universe.
I am grounded in my work and my play.
I remember "how" to play.
It is time to remember.
I am the Light!
I will to play
with you
now
!

Into the great unknown, I leap, into the essence that my mind could not fathom. I come to you bowing in great reverence of all that you know. I come to you humbly for all that you shall show me. I come to you, standing bare naked, innocent, and open to see the expanse that exists. I come to you clean and cleared of what has hindered me, for now I am ready to fully awaken to the nebulous being that I have always been. Show me my Great Unknown Self. Show me how I have always played in the ethers and beyond. Show me how I dance and play within Universes, galaxies, and skies.

Monkey Bars: I can do it!

Do not be led by the imprisoned monkey in the mind. This one is alone and afraid, feeling aggressive and clamoring for a way to be free. Instead, free the monkey mind that it may play in wide-open spaces. Follow this guidance: hear no evil, see no evil, speak no evil. When the monkey mind is set free, it quickly realizes that bars are not to bind but to hold as support while swinging free.

Monkeys climb. Monkeys see. Monkeys do. Monkeys hang by their tails. Monkeys swing through the trees. Monkeys defy gravity. They are intelligent, intense, and involved. They are entertainers, mischievous, and playful. They are compassionate, understanding, and bonding. They are bold and confident, grounded in community. Monkey bars do not limit or bind us. They are not a cage, nor confining. They teach us to maneuver and mount. They allow us to weave in and out, to climb and dance between the lines. Monkey bars give us a structure to follow, but not to be imprisoned within. Monkey bars exist for freedom. Let the monkey mind play freely, but do not get caught in it. Instead talk to the monkey bars, that you may maneuver, play, and discover there are many ways to move about your surroundings.

- When has the monkey mind been alone afraid and trapped? How did you isolate? How did that feel?

- If you were to take those same moments but allowed the monkey mind to venture onto a playground, onto a set of monkey bars, how may have solutions arisen?

- If you allowed the monkey mind to always roam free, how could your true nature rise and swing free?

Trampoline: I can leap as high as I desire!

Trampolines call us. They call something deeply within us, regardless of what age we are. There is something about that feeling of continually leaping that is invigorating and freeing. The more we leap, the higher we go. As we go higher, our arms and hands rise up and wide. We embrace it all. We become adventurous and begin hopping, landing in different positions, doing splits and somersaults. We become boundless, timeless, and free. We are flying. What we never realize is we have become one with the trampoline, the air, and the space in between. All pieces are required for that moment to occur: the spring board, the air, the body, the no-mind, time, and endless possibility. That is Oneness. You are that Oneness. For that to occur, every piece and part of you has to present. Be present and be the present. In that moment you are in Love. You have the courage to keep going higher. You are committed to yourself and the experience. That, in a nutshell, is what life is all about. Never stop leaping with the fullness of Love, Courage, and Commitment!

- How much Love can you stand?

- How much courage can you bring?

- What are you truly committed to?

Invitation From the Author

Who is your world waiting for? You!
What is your world asking for? Your genius!
How will your world be able to have that? Your creativity!

I invite you to become the Rebel, one who is willing to stand in their uniqueness, completely going against what society maybe ready for. It is one who desires to be a pioneer, innovative and creative. The Rebel stands present for an experience. A Rebel's action comes out of their deepest silence and spontaneity. The Rebel only knows adventure, completely alive in the YES that is the precursor to action.

We have been conditioned to believe, think, and feel in restrictive ways about ourselves. Even if the feedback we receive is negative or bogus, we may subconsciously internalize it as truth. We build our lives on these falsities and feed them by subconsciously gravitating toward emotionally unhealthy people and circumstances that validate these distorted messages. You have a question to ask yourself: are you planning to be less than you are capable of? Because the greatest damage is done when you are continuously willing to accept and build on these false, inherited weaknesses.

We have all experienced fear, inhibitions, and self-doubt at one point or another, and ran from, rejected, or avoided an opportunity to change our lives for the better. But continuing to be afraid is a choice. It takes a committed and conscious effort to give yourself permission to stop running and allow the competent, vibrant person inside to take center stage. It will also require mental and emotional muscle to trust yourself to build a newer model that replaces the old one. The good news is right now!

Expect a miracle. Don't just think miracles are possible; know they are. You already have proof of that every single day, but you have denied and overlooked it. You say, "Where is the proof? Where is my everyday miracle?" Well, what do you think you are? Are you not a miracle? Do you not wake up every day? That is your living proof that miracles exist. Not only that, are there not miracles walking all around you? You are that living breathing miracle. So with that truth now self-evident, expect miracles, countless ones. All the time!

Step out of the way and trust. Let your body be the vessel and your voice be the conductor. You are a field of powerful, electrifying Light, Energy, and Sound. Allow others into your Field. Let the Spirit not only rise in you, but also out of you, so that it connects, touches, and expresses to all other parts of itself ready to be in harmony, union, and communion. There is incredible potential lying dormant inside us. You must be clear in your vision, and have unyielding determination and the patience to see all matters to the end. All is wandering.

Are you dreaming while awake? You are, but you are the stranger—a stranger to yourself. Your identity is your lack of identity. Don't be surprised if there are two people in you now: the familiar face that comes and goes through the world, and another face, perhaps one you don't even know yet.

Take the Unknown Road, the Rebel Road. In deep humbleness, great reverence to God-being and absolute respect for you, I ask you to step up and be the Mastery while enjoying this great and Divine Mystery!

Embrace Courage, the Unknown, and Freedom, with Love and Commitment!

In Love, Of Love, With Love, and As Love,

Simran

Afterword

Humanity is in the midst of the most progressive moments ever experienced, since coming into form. Each moment beckons us to step through another accelerated portal of awakening.

We are summoned to entwine ourselves in these extraordinary experiences, in order that we are catapulted beyond the confines of the mundane and ordinary, thus giving ourselves what Joseph Campbell calls, "the privilege of living a truly authentic life."

These expansive occasions allow us to taste the nectar of our True Self, to remember that we are "birthing anew, a level of Light that even the blind will see."

During such occasions we pause for a moment, bending an ear toward a barely audible voice inside, quietly re-minding us that *we* are the Light of Source, the Source of Light that can no longer be denied.

We are the creators that Creator created here, now, to consciously demonstrate the quality and characteristics of One on a "Journey To Enlightenment."

And, there are guiding principles to enhance and connect us to this extraordinary journey. Love. Courage. Commitment. Visionary, author, teacher, and rebel for change Simran Singh knows this journey. She hasn't missed a step. Both her life and the depth of her wisdom reflect that.

There is undeniable power in Simran's words. She uses them as if swords cutting through the illusion of a world that has lived in reverse truth. Overlaying provocative perspective with an invitation for you to flirt with your possibility and freedom, each page nudges you into a world of enlightened reality.

Simran Singh is a guiding Master in our new world and on behalf of our unfolding Divine humanity.

—Maureen Moss, award-winning author,
international teacher of consciousness

Index

A

accepting others, 91

armor, building up your, 69-79

attachments, Rebels and, 95

authentic nature, 29

awareness, 18, 37, 45, 48, 59, 62, 78, 116, 121, 122, 127, 146-154, 160-161, 169, 187-189, 191, 195, 197, 199, 215-216, 228-229, 231, 235

B

beauty, the breath of, 213-214

believing, the importance of, 170-171

belonging, 232-235

binary coding, the Universe and, 134

bondage, 37-49

bonding, 37-49

boundlessness, 230-232

C

calm, finding your, 34-35

celebration, 59, 66-67, 109, 114, 127, 129, 158-160, 182, 189, 229-230

cellular realization, 30

charity, 54

Child, Divine, 109, 151, 154, 156, 185, 194, 213, 217

children,
Divine Confidence and, 157-159
Divine Communication and, 168-169
Divine Guidance and, 177-178
Divine Presence and, 172-174
truth and, 155-156

Communication, Divine, 168-170

conditioning, human, 22, 30, 35

conduct of the Hue-man, 124-128

Confidence, Divine, 157-159

conscious awareness, 190-191

culture of the Hue-man, 116-124

Curiosity, Divine, 159-162

D

death, 125-127, 170, 209, 214, 229

déjà vu, 62

detachment and Divinity, 47-48

Divine Child, 109, 151, 154, 156, 185, 194, 213, 217
  aspects of the, 154

Divine
  Communication, 168-170
  Confidence, 157-159
  Curiosity, 159-162
  Essence, 86, 150-151, 179, 211, 214
  Guidance, 177-178
  Humor, 165-167
  Impulse, 162-164
  Knowing, 49, 93, 120-121
  Light connection, 150
  Love, 178-180
  Mastery, 45
  Nature, 120
  Order, 32, 45
  Path, 133

Presence, 91, 150, 172-174
Self, 58
Simplicity, 174-176
Wisdom, 155-157
Wonder, 152-154

Divinity,
  detachment and, 47-48
  individuation of, 31

dysfunction, 37-38

E

ego, 37-38, 52-53, 88-89, 126, 135, 156, 164

Essence, Divine, 86, 150-151, 179, 211, 214

evolution and involution, 148-149

F

form and formlessness, 227-228

freedom,
  bondage and, 48
  gaining true, 47
  the awakening of, 235-236

frustration, 38-40, 47, 53, 210

G

Gaia, 133-134

genius, unique, 87, 92, 97, 194

gratitude, 40-42, 65, 99-100, 123, 127, 218, 226-227

Guidance, Divine, 177-178

H

heart intelligence, 112-113

human conditioning, 22, 30, 35

Humor, Divine, 165-167

I

identity, clinging to an, 35

illumination, 134, 145, 194, 217, 225-239

illusion, magic and, 130

Impulse, Divine, 162-164

innocence, breath of 211-213

intelligence, heart, 112-113

involution and evolution, 148-149

L

language of the Hue-man, 109-115

life purpose, 39, 122

Light Being, 225, 231, 235

Light body, 31

Love,
Divine, 178-180
unconditional, 69, 109, 155, 198, 216, 231

M

magic and illusion, 130

Mastery,
awakening to your, 34-35
being in service to your, 52

material things, craving, 43-45

N

neurological network, 133-134

New Dawn, 24, 112, 120, 127, 194, 196, 208
death and the, 127
moving into the, 208-209

non-identity, Divine Wisdom and, 156

O

Oneness, the breath of, 216-217
Ones of Light, 225

P

past language, 111
power, false sense of, 38
praise, receiving and giving, 89
Presence, Divine, 91, 150, 172-174
purpose of life, 122-123

R

realization, cellular, 30
Rebel, becoming the, 33-34
Rebels, 120
    control and, 93-94
    travels of, 94-95
restlessness, 38-39, 47, 53

S

sadness, 43, 64, 121, 127
Self, love and the greater, 88
self-love, steps of, 108
service, 49-68

servitude, 49-68
Simplicity, Divine, 174-176
stress, modern-day, 30
subconscious, support from
    the, 119
surprise, enjoying the element
    of, 101-102

T

timelessness, 225, 228-230, 232
Torus energy system, 112, 128
transformation, 192-194
transmutation, 192-194
transparency, 70, 78, 138,
    195, 215,
Truth Self, 64
truth,
    children and, 155-156
    living your, 89

U

Universe,
    being thrown into the, 15
    benevolent, 48
    binary coding and the, 134
    conversations with the, 18, 20,
        59, 95, 159, 171, 197, 229

Divine Children of the, 151
elements of the, 195
law of the, 133
mystery of the, 129
natural order of the, 196
nature of the, 114
physical body and the, 188
realignment and the, 148

W

Wisdom, Divine, 155-157
Wonder, Divine, 152-154

About the Author

Simran Singh is a creative visionary, transformational catalyst, and "Leading Voice for the Journey of the Soul." Publisher of the Nautilus Award–Winning *11:11 Magazine*, the only publication to have ever been granted this designation, and number-one rated, syndicated 11:11 Talk Radio show host, Simran brings to the forefront a unique interpretation, blending co-creative power with metaphysics and personal responsibility.

As author of *Your Journey To Enlightenment* and *Conversations With The Universe*, and Lead Rebel of The Rebel Road Tour, Simran impacts thousands upon thousands with her message. Her passionate style takes individuals on a journey into personal power, authenticity, and presence through writing, speaking, blogging, and creative expression as the Rebel in her one-woman show, *The Rebel Road: Connecting the Dots of What Was to What IS*.

Simran's Content Sites and Contact

www.Simran-Singh.com

www.1111mag.com

www.TheRebelRoad.com

Simran's Book Sites and Free Tools

www.SimransBooks.com

www.YourJourneyToEnlightenment.com

www.ConversationsWithTheUniverse.com

Social Media Links

Facebook:

www.facebook.com/1111Magazine

www.facebook.com/SimranSingh1111

www.facebook.com/TheRebelRoad

Twitter

https://twitter.com/1111Magazine

https://twitter.com/SimranSingh1111

LinkedIn

www.linkedin.com/in/SimranSingh1111

Pinterest

http://Pinterest.com/SimranSingh1111

YouTube Daily Diaries and Features

www.youtube.com/SimranSingh1111

Email: Simran@Simran-Singh.com